diabetic LIVING Everyday COOKING

VOLUME 3

DIABETIC LIVING® EVERYDAY COOKING IS
PART OF A BOOK SERIES PUBLISHED BY
BETTER HOMES AND GARDENS SPECIAL
INTEREST MEDIA, DES MOINES, IOWA

Pineapple-Turkey Kabobs
recipe, page 27

Letter from the Editor

My husband and I both work outside the home, and our Son, Grant, grows taller every day. So I look for opportunities to carve a few more minutes out of each day to enjoy family activities. I've found that by simply enlisting help from my son and husband with household chores, we do have time to play a game or watch a movie.

Grant enjoys helping in the kitchen, and we've spent some great moments preparing meals. Whether we're stirring together a creamy dip for a snack, rolling turkey and veggies in wraps for lunch, or chopping and dicing vegetables and meat for a stir-fried dinner, I treasure the opportunity to teach him the basics of good nutrition.

As a person with type 1 diabetes, I know that nutritious food helps me control my condition and feel good. That's why I turn to this collection of healthful recipes to help fuel my meal plan as well as nourish my family. The recipes have been perfected in the Better Homes and Gardens® Test Kitchen. That's why I know each dish will turn out great and taste delicious every time I serve it.

Because our Test Kitchen staff includes registered dietitians, I can count on each recipe to deliver healthful amounts of calories, carbs, and sodium. They keep an eye on ingredients—not too many and not too exotic. And they try to use convenience products such as canned reduced-sodium chicken broth that help to save me time and to cook with my health in mind.

Reach for this collection day after day for satisfying meals—breakfast, lunch, dinner, and snacks. You'll find you can stop worrying about what to eat and start enjoying time with your family.

Kelly Rawlings

Kelly Rawlings, PWD type 1
Editor, *Diabetic Living*® magazine

ON THE COVER:
Meatball Lasagna
(recipe, page 13)
Photographer: Scott Little
Food stylist: Jennifer Petersen

CONSUMER MARKETING

Vice President, Consumer Marketing	DAVID BALL
Consumer Product Marketing Director	STEVE SWANSON
Consumer Product Marketing Manager	WENDY MERICAL
Business Director	RON CLINGMAN
Associate Director, Production	DOUGLAS M. JOHNSTON

Contributing Editorial Director	SHELLI MCCONNELL
Contributing Design Director	JILL BUDDEN
Contributing Copy Editor	GRETCHEN KAUFFMAN
Contributing Proofreader	CARRIE SCHMITZ
Test Kitchen Director	LYNN BLANCHARD
Test Kitchen Product Supervisor	LAURA MARZEN, R.D.
Editorial Assistants	LORI EGGERS, MARLENE TODD

DIABETIC LIVING® MAGAZINE

Editor in Chief	DEBORAH GORE OHRN
Executive Editor	BRIDGET SANDQUIST
Editor	KELLY RAWLINGS
Art Director	MICHELLE BILYEU
Design Director	TERESA LAURENZO

MEREDITH PUBLISHING GROUP

President JACK GRIFFIN

Executive Vice President ANDY SAREYAN

Vice President, Manufacturing BRUCE HESTON

President and Chief Executive Officer STEPHEN M. LACY

Chairman of the Board WILLIAM T. KERR

In Memoriam — E.T. MEREDITH III (1933-2003)

Diabetic Living® Everyday Cooking Volume 3 is part of a series published by Meredith Corp., 1716 Locust St., Des Moines, IA 50309-3023.

If you have comments or questions about the editorial material in *Diabetic Living® Everyday Cooking Volume 3*, write to the editor of *Diabetic Living®* magazine, Meredith Corp., 1716 Locust St., Des Moines, IA 50309-3023. Send an e-mail to diabeticliving@meredith.com or call 800/678-2651. *Diabetic Living®* magazine is available by subscription or on the newsstand. To order a subscription to *Diabetic Living®* magazine, go to *DiabeticLivingOnline.com*.

ISSN 1943-2615   ISBN 978-0-696-24390-5

If you're looking to perk up your weekday dinner menus, turn to these palate pleasers. You'll find a selection of quick-to-fix, slow-simmered, bubbly baked, and hot-off-the-grill dishes, all packed with delicious taste and good-for-you ingredients.

Herb-Garlic Beef Roast

With a little help from of a precooked beef roast and microwave-cooked veggies, this comfort-food classic is on the table in less than 20 minutes.

SERVINGS 4
CARB. PER SERVING 28 g

1 17-ounce package refrigerated cooked beef roast au jus
1 pound small round red potatoes
3 medium carrots
1 tablespoon canola oil
Black pepper
3 tablespoons chopped fresh Italian (flat-leaf) parsley
3 to 6 cloves garlic, minced
1 tablespoon finely shredded lemon peel

1. In a large skillet, cook beef roast, covered, over medium heat for 10 minutes. Uncover and simmer about 5 minutes more or until juices are slightly reduced.
2. Meanwhile, quarter potatoes. Peel and diagonally slice carrots in ¾-inch pieces. Place vegetables in a microwave-safe dish. Drizzle with oil and sprinkle with pepper; toss to coat. Tightly cover with lid or plastic wrap. Microwave on high (100% power) for 10 minutes or until tender.
3. For herb-garlic mixture: In a small bowl, combine parsley, garlic, and lemon peel. To serve, stir vegetables into skillet with beef and juices. Divide among serving dishes. Sprinkle with herb-garlic mixture.

PER SERVING: 311 cal., 12 g total fat (5 g sat. fat), 64 mg chol., 465 mg sodium, 28 g carb., 4 g fiber, 25 g pro. Exchanges: 0.5 vegetable, 1.5 starch, 3 lean meat, 1 fat. Carb choices: 2.

Sweet and Spicy
Edamame-Beef Stir-Fry

Sweet and Spicy Edamame-Beef Stir-Fry

*Look for the hoisin sauce, rice vinegar, and red chile paste
in the Asian foods section of your supermarket.*

SERVINGS 4 (about ¾ cup stir-fry mixture and
½ cup rice each)

CARB. PER SERVING 34 g

- 4 teaspoons canola oil
- 2 teaspoons finely chopped fresh ginger
- 3 cups packaged fresh cut-up stir-fry vegetables
- 8 ounces boneless beef sirloin steak, trimmed of fat and cut in very thin bite-size strips
- 1 cup frozen shelled sweet soybeans (edamame)
- 3 tablespoons hoisin sauce
- 2 tablespoons rice vinegar
- 1 teaspoon red chile paste
- 1 8.8-ounce pouch cooked whole grain brown rice

1. In a nonstick wok or skillet, heat half of the oil
over medium-high heat. Add ginger; stir-fry for
15 seconds. Add vegetables; stir-fry about 4 minutes
or until crisp-tender. Remove vegetables.
2. Add remaining oil to wok. Add beef and edamame to
wok; stir-fry about 2 minutes or until beef is browned.
Return vegetables to wok. In a small bowl, stir together
hoisin sauce, vinegar, and chile paste. Add to beef
mixture, tossing to coat. Heat through.
3. Meanwhile, heat rice according to package directions.
Serve beef mixture over rice.

PER SERVING: 330 cal., 12 g total fat (2 g sat. fat), 24 mg chol.,
272 mg sodium, 34 g carb., 5 g fiber, 22 g pro. Exchanges:
1 vegetable, 2 starch, 2.5 lean meat, 0.5 fat. Carb
choices: 2.

Flat Iron Steak with BBQ Beans

To cut back on carbs, choose a low-carb barbecue sauce.

SERVINGS 4 (½ steak and ⅓ cup beans each)

CARB. PER SERVING 25 g

- 2 boneless beef shoulder top blade (flat iron) steaks, halved (1 to 1¼ pounds total)
- 2 teaspoons fajita seasoning
- 1 15-ounce can black beans, rinsed and drained
- ⅓ cup bottled barbecue sauce
- 2 to 3 tomatoes, sliced
  Pickled jalapeño pepper slices (optional)

1. Grease a grill pan. Preheat grill pan over medium-
high heat. Sprinkle steaks with fajita seasoning. On
the greased grill pan, grill steaks for 8 to 12 minutes
for medium-rare doneness (145°F) or 12 to 15 minutes
for medium doneness (160°F).
2. Meanwhile, in a medium microwave-safe bowl, stir
together beans and barbecue sauce. Cover loosely with
plastic wrap. Microwave on high (100% power) for
3 minutes, stirring once.
3. Serve steaks with sliced tomatoes and beans. If
desired, top with pickled jalapeño pepper slices.

PER SERVING: 303 cal., 11 g total fat (4 g sat. fat), 74 mg chol.,
638 mg sodium, 25 g carb., 6 g fiber, 29 g pro. Exchanges:
0.5 vegetable, 1.5 starch, 3.5 lean meat. Carb choices: 1.5.

Dijon-Pepper Steak

Pepper steak is a classic French dish that starts with meat coated with cracked black pepper and finishes with an easy-to-make sauce. This simple slow-cooker version follows that basic plan.

SERVINGS 6 (about 3 ounces meat and scant ½ cup sauce-vegetable mixture each)

CARB. PER SERVING 10 g

- 2 pounds boneless beef sirloin steak, cut 1 inch thick
- 1 to 1½ teaspoons cracked black pepper
- 1 tablespoon canola oil
- 2 cups packaged whole trimmed baby carrots
- 1 medium onion, sliced
- 1 10.75-ounce can reduced-fat and reduced-sodium condensed cream of celery soup
- 2 tablespoons Dijon-style mustard
- 3 cups hot cooked multigrain penne pasta (optional)

Snipped fresh parsley (optional)

1. Trim fat from steak. Cut steak into six serving-size pieces. Sprinkle cracked pepper evenly over meat; press in with your fingers. In a large skillet, brown meat, half at a time, in hot oil. Drain off fat. Set aside.

2. Place carrots and onion in a 3½- or 4-quart slow cooker. Add meat. In a medium bowl, stir together cream of celery soup and Dijon-style mustard. Pour over mixture in cooker.

3. Cover and cook on low-heat setting for 7 to 8 hours or on high-heat setting for 3½ to 4 hours. If desired, before serving, use a fork to slightly break up meat pieces. If desired, serve over hot cooked pasta and garnish with parsley.

PER SERVING: 275 cal., 9 g total fat (3 g sat. fat), 65 mg chol., 410 mg sodium, 10 g carb., 1 g fiber, 34 g pro. Exchanges: 1 vegetable, 4.5 lean meat. Carb choices: 0.5.

Grilled Marinated Flank Steak

doneness (160°F). (For a gas grill, preheat grill. Reduce heat to medium. Place meat on grill rack over heat. Cover and grill as at left.)

3. Thinly slice meat against the grain. Serve meat in flour tortillas with the shredded lettuce, Sweet Pepper Salsa, Artichoke-Bean Spread, and/or Quick Steak Sauce.

PER SERVING: 290 cal., 9 g total fat (3 g sat. fat), 28 mg chol., 509 mg sodium, 22 g carb., 11 g fiber, 27 g pro. Exchanges: 1.5 starch, 3 lean meat, 1 fat. Carb choices: 1.5.

SWEET PEPPER SALSA: In a medium bowl, toss together 2 medium green and/or yellow sweet peppers, finely chopped; 1 fresh serrano chile pepper, seeded and chopped (see tip, page 32); ½ cup finely chopped, peeled jicama; ¼ cup finely chopped red onion; 2 tablespoons snipped fresh cilantro; 1 tablespoon red wine vinegar; and ¼ teaspoon salt. Cover and chill. Makes about 2½ cups.

PER TABLESPOON: 3 cal., 0 g total fat, 0 mg chol., 15 mg sodium, 1 g carb., 0 g fiber, 0 g pro. Exchanges: 0. Carb choices: 0.

ARTICHOKE-BEAN SPREAD: Drain one 6-ounce jar marinated artichoke hearts, reserving marinade. Coarsely chop artichokes and set aside. In a food processor,* combine the marinade from artichoke hearts; one 15-ounce can garbanzo beans, rinsed and drained; 2 tablespoons thinly sliced green onion; and 1 tablespoon finely shredded lemon peel. Cover and process until smooth. Stir in artichokes. Stir in ⅛ teaspoon salt and ⅛ teaspoon black pepper. Cover and chill for up to 3 days. Makes about 2 cups.

***TEST KITCHEN TIP:** If you don't have a food processor, mash garbanzo beans with a potato masher, gradually adding the artichoke marinade. Stir in sliced green onion, lemon peel, and artichokes. Stir in salt and pepper.

PER TABLESPOON: 26 cal., 1 g total fat (0 g sat. fat), 0 mg chol., 67 mg sodium, 3 g carb., 1 g fiber, 1 g pro. Exchanges: 0.5 fat. Carb choices: 0.

QUICK STEAK SAUCE: In a blender, combine ¼ cup red wine vinegar, ¼ cup chopped onion, ¼ cup raisins, 2 tablespoons tomato paste, 1 tablespoon molasses, 1 tablespoon packed brown sugar, 1 tablespoon reduced-sodium soy sauce, and ¼ teaspoon black pepper. Cover and blend until nearly smooth. Cover and store in refrigerator for up to 1 week. Makes about ¾ cup.

PER TABLESPOON: 24 cal., 0 g total fat, 0 mg chol., 67 mg sodium, 6 g carb., 0 g fiber, 0 g pro. Exchanges: 0.5 carb. Carb choices: 0.5.

Grilled Marinated Flank Steak

Take your pick—three great condiments to choose from.

SERVINGS 4 (4 ounces steak, 1 tortilla, and 1 tablespoon Sweet Pepper Salsa each)

CARB. PER SERVING 22 g

- 1 12-ounce beef flank steak
- 3 tablespoons red wine vinegar
- 1 large clove garlic, minced
- 1 tablespoon Dijon-style mustard
- 1 tablespoon snipped fresh cilantro
- ⅛ teaspoon crushed red pepper
- 4 8-inch whole wheat tortillas
     Shredded lettuce
- ½ cup Sweet Pepper Salsa, Artichoke-Bean Spread, and/ or Quick Steak Sauce (right)

1. Trim fat from steak. Score steak on both sides by making shallow diagonal cuts at 1-inch intervals in a diamond pattern. Place meat in a resealable plastic bag set in a shallow dish; set aside. In a small bowl, stir together the vinegar, garlic, mustard, cilantro, and red pepper until well combined. Pour over meat in bag. Seal bag; turn to coat meat. Marinate in the refrigerator for 30 minutes. Drain meat, discarding marinade.

2. For a charcoal grill, place meat on the grill rack directly over medium coals. Grill, uncovered, until desired doneness. Allow 14 to 17 minutes for medium-rare doneness (145°F) or 17 to 21 minutes for medium

Flank Steak with Corn Salsa

Draining away and discarding the marinade rather than brushing it on during grilling helps keep this fresh-tasting flank steak low in fat.

SERVINGS 6 (3 ounces steak and ¼ cup salsa each)
CARB. PER SERVING 9 g

- 1 8.75-ounce can whole kernel corn, drained
- ¾ cup bottled salsa verde
- 1 medium tomato, chopped
- 1 1¼- to 1½-pound beef flank steak
- ¾ cup bottled reduced-calorie clear Italian salad dressing
- 2 tablespoons cracked black pepper
- 1 tablespoon Worcestershire sauce
- 1 teaspoon ground cumin

1. For corn salsa: In a medium bowl, combine corn, salsa verde, and tomato. Cover and chill for 6 to 24 hours.

2. Meanwhile, trim fat from steak. Score both sides of steak in a diamond pattern by making shallow diagonal cuts at 1-inch intervals. Place meat in a resealable plastic bag set in a shallow dish.

3. For marinade: In a small bowl, combine Italian salad dressing, pepper, Worcestershire sauce, and cumin; pour over meat. Seal bag; turn to coat meat. Marinate in the refrigerator for 6 to 24 hours, turning bag occasionally. Drain meat, discarding marinade.

4. For a charcoal grill, place meat on the grill rack directly over medium coals. Grill, uncovered, until desired doneness. Allow 14 to 17 minutes for medium-rare doneness (145°F) or 17 to 21 minutes for medium doneness (160°F). (For a gas grill, preheat grill. Reduce heat to medium. Place meat on grill rack over heat. Cover and grill as above.)

5. To serve, thinly slice meat diagonally across the grain. Serve meat with corn salsa.

PER SERVING: 193 cal., 8 g total fat (3 g sat. fat), 39 mg chol., 352 mg sodium, 9 g carb., 1 g fiber, 22 g pro. Exchanges: 0.5 vegetable, 0.5 starch, 2.5 lean meat. Carb choices: 0.5.

Flank Steak with Corn Salsa

Gold Medal Moussaka

Gold Medal Moussaka

Low-fat products lighten this classic Greek specialty.

SERVINGS 4 (1 au gratin dish each)
CARB. PER SERVING 18 g

Nonstick cooking spray

1 1-pound eggplant, peeled (if desired) and cut into ¾-inch cubes

8 ounces lean ground beef or ground lamb

1 8-ounce can tomato sauce with basil, garlic, and oregano

⅛ teaspoon ground cinnamon

2 tablespoons flour

2 tablespoons olive oil

¼ teaspoon salt

Dash black pepper

½ cup fat-free milk

½ cup plain low-fat yogurt

½ cup light ricotta cheese

⅓ cup refrigerated or frozen egg product, thawed

Ground cinnamon

Parmesan cheese, thinly sliced (optional)

1. Preheat oven to 350°F. Lightly coat a very large nonstick skillet with cooking spray; heat over medium-high heat. Add eggplant; cook about 6 minutes or until tender, stirring frequently. Set aside.

2. Meanwhile, in a large skillet, cook ground meat until browned. Drain off fat. Stir in tomato sauce and the ⅛ teaspoon cinnamon. Bring to boiling; reduce heat. Simmer, uncovered, about 8 minutes or until sauce thickens, stirring occasionally. Divide meat mixture among four individual 12- to 14-ounce au gratin or baking dishes. Top with eggplant.

3. In a small saucepan, combine flour, oil, salt, and pepper. Add milk and yogurt all at once. Cook and stir over medium heat until thickened and bubbly; remove from heat. Stir in ricotta cheese. Stir in egg product. Spoon cheese mixture on top of eggplant. Sprinkle lightly with additional ground cinnamon.

4. Bake, uncovered, about 25 minutes or until heated through. If desired, top with Parmesan. Let stand 5 minutes before serving.

PER SERVING: 280 cal., 14 g total fat (4 g sat. fat), 47 mg chol., 582 mg sodium, 18 g carb., 4 g fiber, 20 g pro. Exchanges: 2.5 vegetable, 2.5 medium-fat meat, 1.5 fat. Carb choices: 1.

Mediterranean Meatballs

Use these in Meatball Lasagna or serve them in whole wheat pita halves with a little purchased marinara sauce.
SERVINGS 8 (3 meatballs each)
CARB. PER SERVING 2

- ½ cup bottled roasted red peppers, drained and finely chopped
- ¾ cup soft whole wheat bread crumbs (about 1 slice)
- ¼ cup refrigerated or frozen egg product, thawed, or 1 egg, lightly beaten
- 3 tablespoons purchased tomato sauce
- ¼ cup snipped fresh basil
- 2 tablespoons snipped fresh Italian (flat-leaf) parsley
- 1 pound 95%-lean ground beef
   Snipped fresh Italian (flat-leaf) parsley

1. Preheat oven to 350°F. In a large bowl, combine the roasted red peppers, the bread crumbs, egg, tomato sauce, basil, the 2 tablespoons parsley, ¼ teaspoon *salt*, and ⅛ teaspoon *black pepper*. Add ground beef; mix well.
2. Line a 15×10×1-inch baking pan with foil. Shape meat mixture into 24 meatballs. Place meatballs in prepared baking pan. Bake about 20 minutes or until done (160°F).* Transfer meatballs to a tray. Use meatballs to make the Meatball Lasagna.
***TEST KITCHEN TIP:** The internal color of meatballs is not a reliable doneness indicator. A beef meatball cooked to 160°F is safe, regardless of color. To measure the doneness of a meatball, insert an instant-read thermometer into the center of the ball.
PER SERVING: 94 cal., 3 g total fat, (1 g sat. fat), 35 mg chol., 170 mg sodium, 2 g carb., 1 g fiber, 14 g pro. Exchanges: 2 lean meat. Carb choices: 0.

Meatball Lasagna

Mediterranean Meatballs do double duty for this lasagna.
SERVINGS 8 (1 piece)
CARB. PER SERVING 22 g

- 2 medium green sweet peppers, stemmed, seeded, and quartered
- 6 dried regular or whole wheat lasagna noodles
- 1½ cups shredded reduced-fat mozzarella cheese (6 ounces)
- ½ of a 15-ounce container (¾ cup) light ricotta cheese
- ¼ cup soft goat cheese (chèvre) or finely shredded Parmesan cheese (1 ounce)
- 1½ cups purchased light or low-fat tomato basil pasta sauce
- ½ recipe cooked Mediterranean Meatballs (24)
   Shredded fresh basil or small fresh basil or oregano leaves (optional)

1. Preheat oven to 425°F. Line a large baking sheet with foil. Place sweet pepper quarters, cut sides down, on prepared baking sheet. Roast, uncovered, about 20 minutes or until pepper quarters are charred. Wrap in the foil; let stand for 20 minutes. Using a small sharp knife, peel skins from pepper quarters. Set aside. Reduce oven temperature to 375°F.
2. Meanwhile, cook lasagna noodles according to package directions. Drain noodles; rinse with cold water. Drain well; set aside. For filling: In a small bowl, stir together 1 cup of the mozzarella cheese, the ricotta cheese, and the goat cheese or Parmesan cheese; set aside.
3. To assemble, spread ½ cup of the pasta sauce in the bottom of a 2-quart rectangular baking dish. Layer two of the cooked noodles in the dish. Arrange meatballs in a single layer on top of noodles in dish. Add two more of the cooked noodles. Top with the ricotta cheese mixture, spreading evenly. Arrange sweet pepper pieces over ricotta mixture. Top with the remaining cooked noodles. Spread the remaining pasta sauce over noodles.
4. Bake, covered, for 50 minutes. Uncover and sprinkle with the remaining ½ cup mozzarella cheese. Bake, uncovered, for 5 to 10 minutes more or until heated through. Let stand for 15 minutes before serving. Cut into 8 pieces. If desired, garnish with fresh herbs.
PER SERVING: 262 cal., 8 g total fat, (4 g sat. fat), 54 mg chol., 471 mg sodium, 22 g carb., 2 g fiber, 23 g pro. Exchanges: 0.5 vegetable, 1.5 starch, 2.5 lean meat, 0.5 fat. Carb choices: 1.5.

Meatball Lasagna

Curried Pork and Rice

3. Bake, covered, about 45 minutes or until rice is tender and most of the liquid is absorbed. Let stand, covered, on a wire rack for 5 minutes. Sprinkle with peanuts and cilantro before serving.

PER SERVING: 275 cal., 7 g total fat (2 g sat. fat), 56 mg chol., 289 mg sodium, 27 g carb., 3 g fiber, 25 g pro. Exchanges: 0.5 milk, 1.5 starch, 2.5 lean meat. Carb choices: 2.

Pork Chops Primavera

Apple butter and water make a sweet, fruity glaze for these quick-cooking chops.

SERVINGS 4 (1 chop and about 1½ cups vegetable mixture each)

CARB. PER SERVING 26 g

- 2 slices turkey bacon, cut into 1-inch pieces
- 12 ounces trimmed fresh young green beans
- 4 pork rib chops, cut ½ inch thick (about 1½ pounds total)
- 1 tablespoon reduced-sodium soy sauce
- 2 teaspoons canola oil
- 3 tablespoons apple butter
- 1 cup red and/or yellow cherry and/or grape tomatoes

1. In a very large nonstick skillet, cook bacon according to package directions. Remove from skillet; set aside.
2. Meanwhile, in a 2-quart microwave-safe dish, combine beans and 2 tablespoons *water*. Cover with lid or plastic wrap. Microwave on high (100% power) for 4 minutes, stirring once. Drain and set aside.
3. Brush chops with soy sauce. In the same skillet, brown chops on both sides in hot oil over medium heat. Add apple butter and 3 tablespoons *water*; reduce heat. Simmer, covered, for 5 minutes. Add beans, tomatoes, and cooked bacon. Cook, uncovered, for 3 to 5 minutes or until heated through.

PER SERVING: 307 cal., 7 g total fat (3 g sat. fat), 83 mg chol., 309 mg sodium, 26 g carb., 4 g fiber, 33 g pro. Exchanges: 1 vegetable, 1.5 carb., 4 lean meat. Carb choices: 2.

Curried Pork and Rice

Seasoning the pork and rice with a low-fat curry sauce, tart apple, and fresh cilantro means this hearty dish is loaded with flavor but still fits into a sensible meal plan.

SERVINGS 4 (about 1 cup each)

CARB. PER SERVING 27 g

- 1 teaspoon canola oil
- 12 ounces boneless pork loin, cut into thin bite-size strips
- 2 cups fat-free milk
- 2 tablespoons all-purpose flour
- 1½ teaspoons curry powder
- ¼ teaspoon salt
- ¾ cup instant brown rice
- 1 medium green apple (such as Granny Smith), cored and chopped
- 1 medium carrot, coarsely shredded
- 3 green onions, bias-sliced
- 2 tablespoons chopped peanuts
- 2 tablespoons snipped fresh cilantro

1. Preheat oven to 350°F. In a large nonstick skillet, heat oil over medium heat. Add pork; cook for 3 to 5 minutes or until done. Drain off fat. Set aside.
2. In a screw-top jar, combine ½ cup of the milk, the flour, curry powder, and salt; cover and shake until well mixed. Transfer to a medium saucepan; add remaining milk. Cook and stir over medium heat until thickened and bubbly. Stir in pork, uncooked rice, apple, carrot, and green onions. Transfer to a 1½-quart casserole. Place casserole on a baking sheet.

QUICK TIP ◖

Fresh green beans cook in a snap when you trim off the stem ends and leave them whole. Sometimes thin young beans are hard to find, so allow a few minutes more for cooking thicker beans.

Pork Chops Primavera

Chops and Pineapple
with Chili Slaw

Chops and Pineapple with Chili Slaw

Another day, treat yourself to a tropical fruit dessert using the remaining pineapple half. Cut it into pieces and sprinkle with a few toasted macadamia nuts or shredded coconut.

SERVINGS 4 (2 chops and about 1¾ cups slaw each)
CARB. PER SERVING 20 g

8	boneless pork top loin chops, cut ½ inch thick (about 1½ pounds total)
1½	teaspoons chili powder
½	of a cored fresh pineapple, sliced
3	tablespoons cider vinegar
2	tablespoons orange juice
2	tablespoons olive oil
1	tablespoon sugar
⅓	of a small green cabbage, cored and sliced (about 5 cups)
½	of a red onion, thinly sliced
1	small red sweet pepper, cut into strips

1. Sprinkle chops with *salt* and 1 teaspoon of the chili powder. For a charcoal grill, place chops and pineapple slices on the grill rack directly over medium coals. Grill, uncovered, for 6 to 8 minutes or until chops are done (160°F), turning once. (For a gas grill, preheat grill. Reduce heat to medium. Place chops and pineapple slices on grill rack over heat. Cover and grill as above.)

2. Meanwhile, for chili slaw: In a large bowl, whisk together vinegar, orange juice, oil, sugar, and remaining ½ teaspoon chili powder. Add cabbage, onion, and sweet pepper; toss to coat. Season with *salt* and *black pepper*. Serve chops with pineapple pieces and slaw.

PER SERVING: 357 cal., 12 g total fat (3 g sat. fat), 112 mg chol., 392 mg sodium, 20 g carb., 4 g fiber, 40 g pro. Exchanges: 1.5 vegetable, 1 fruit, 5 lean meat, 0.5 fat. Carb choices: 1.

Pork Chops Pizziola

Snipped oregano leaves add a refreshing note to the tomato sauce. Another time, make it using fresh basil.

SERVINGS 4 (1 chop and 1/3 cup sauce each)
CARB. PER SERVING 7 g

- 4 pork rib chops, cut 1/2 inch thick (about 1 1/2 pounds total)
- 1 tablespoon canola oil
- 2 cloves garlic, minced
- 1 tablespoon snipped fresh oregano or 1 teaspoon dried oregano, crushed
- 1 14.5-ounce can no-salt-added diced tomatoes, undrained
- 1/4 cup dry red wine or low-sodium tomato juice
- 1 tablespoon tomato paste

1. Trim fat from pork chops. In a large skillet, heat oil over medium-high heat. Cook the chops in hot oil for 4 to 6 minutes or until evenly browned, turning once. Remove from skillet; set aside.

2. Add garlic and dried oregano (if using) to skillet; cook and stir for 15 seconds. Add undrained tomatoes, red wine, and tomato paste; stir to combine. Bring to boiling; reduce heat.

3. Return pork chops to skillet. Cover and simmer for 30 minutes. Transfer chops to a serving dish. Skim any fat from sauce. Stir fresh oregano (if using) into sauce. If desired, cook sauce, uncovered, for 1 to 2 minutes more or until desired consistency, stirring occasionally.

PER SERVING: 210 cal., 10 g total fat (3 g sat. fat), 58 mg chol., 130 mg sodium, 7 g carb., 2 g fiber, 19 g pro. Exchanges: 1 vegetable, 2.5 lean meat, 1 fat. Carb choices: 0.5.

Pork Chops Pizziola

Citrus and Spice Pork Chops

If you wish, use medium skinless, boneless chicken breast halves instead of the chops. Cook the chicken for 12 to 15 minutes or until done (170°F), turning once.

SERVINGS 4 (1 chop each)
CARB. PER SERVING 20 g

- 4 boneless pork loin chops, cut 1/2 inch thick (about 1 1/2 pounds total)
- 3 tablespoons orange juice or grapefruit juice
- 2 teaspoons Jamaican jerk or Montreal steak seasoning
- 1 tablespoon canola oil
- 2 tablespoons Dijon-style mustard
- 1/3 cup orange marmalade
- 1/4 cup chopped roasted cashews or peanuts (optional)

1. Brush both sides of pork chops with 1 tablespoon of the orange juice. Sprinkle both sides with seasoning. In a large nonstick skillet, cook chops in hot oil over medium heat for 9 to 11 minutes or until slightly pink in the center (160°F), turning once halfway through cooking. Transfer chops to a platter.

2. Remove pan from heat. Stir mustard into pan drippings. Whisk in marmalade and remaining 2 tablespoons orange juice. Return to heat. Cook and stir just until boiling. Pour sauce over chops. If desired, sprinkle with nuts.

PER SERVING: 342 cal., 11 g total fat (3 g sat. fat), 107 mg chol., 435 mg sodium, 20 g carb., 0 g fiber, 39 g pro. Exchanges: 1 carb., 5.5 lean meat, 0.5 fat. Carb choices: 1.

Orange and Rosemary
Pork Chops

Cherry-Kissed Tacos
with Feta Cheese Salsa

Garlic-Chili-Rubbed Lamb
recipe on page 20

Lighten Up

If you think some of your treasured
recipes are now off limits, think again.
Use these makeover tips to lighten
your own main-dish recipes
at home.

1. **Use low-fat and fat-free
   dairy products** in place of
   full-fat options.

2. **Swap high-sodium, high-
   fat meats** such as ham and
   pepperoni for lean meats
   with no added salt.

3. **Choose ground turkey or
   chicken breast** instead of
   ground beef or pork.

4. **Use reduced-sodium sauces,**
   broths, and soups.

5. **Coat a skillet with nonstick
   cooking spray** instead of oil
   for sautéing.

6. **Use fresh produce** instead of
   canned, which is higher
   in sodium.

7. **Try whole grain pasta** as a
   substitute for regular pasta.

8. **Reach for refrigerated or
   frozen egg product** or egg
   whites instead of whole eggs.

Orange and Rosemary Pork Chops

Molasses comes in three strengths: Mild-flavor molasses is lightest in color, blackstrap is very dark—and very strong, and full-flavor is somewhere in the middle. For more molasses flavor, use the full-flavor or blackstrap variety in this recipe.

SERVINGS 4 (1 chop each)
CARB. PER SERVING 3 g

- 4 4- to 5-ounce boneless pork loin chops, cut 1 inch thick
- 2 teaspoons finely shredded orange peel
- ½ cup orange juice
- 2 tablespoons snipped fresh rosemary or 2 teaspoons dried rosemary, crushed
- 2 tablespoons Worcestershire-style marinade for chicken
- 1 tablespoon olive oil
- 1 tablespoon mild-flavor molasses or maple syrup
- ⅛ teaspoon black pepper
- 2 cups orange, apple, or peach wood chips or 6 orange, apple, or peach wood chunks
   Fresh rosemary sprigs (optional)

1. Trim fat from chops. Place chops in a large resealable plastic bag set in a shallow dish. For marinade: In a small bowl, combine orange peel, orange juice, the snipped or dried rosemary, Worcestershire-style marinade, olive oil, molasses, and pepper.
2. Pour marinade over chops. Seal bag; turn to coat chops. Marinate in the refrigerator for 4 to 24 hours, turning bag occasionally.
3. At least 1 hour before grilling, soak wood chips or chunks in enough water to cover. Drain before using. Drain chops, reserving marinade.
4. Arrange medium-hot coals around a drip pan. Test for medium heat above the pan. Sprinkle the drained wood chips or chunks over the coals. Place chops on the grill rack over drip pan. Cover and grill for 20 to 24 minutes or until pork is slightly pink in the center (160°F), brushing once with marinade halfway through grilling. Discard any remaining marinade. If desired, garnish with rosemary sprigs.
PER SERVING: 178 cal., 6 g total fat (2 g sat. fat), 62 mg chol., 86 mg sodium, 3 g carb., 0 g fiber, 25 g pro. Exchanges: 3.5 lean meat, 0.5 fat. Carb choices: 0.

Cherry-Kissed Tacos with Feta Cheese Salsa

These are great for a party—this fruity version of the taco will have guests asking for more.

SERVINGS 12 (1 taco and 2 tablespoons salsa each)
CARB. PER SERVING 21 g

- 1 pound lean ground lamb or ground pork
- 1 cup finely chopped onion
- 1 teaspoon curry powder
- ½ cup mango chutney
- ½ cup dried tart red cherries, chopped
- 1 tablespoon lemon juice
- ¼ teaspoon salt
- ¼ teaspoon black pepper
- 12 taco shells, warmed
- 1 recipe Feta Cheese Salsa (below)

1. In a large skillet, cook ground meat and onion until meat is browned and onion is tender. Drain off fat. Add curry powder; cook and stir for 1 minute.
2. Cut up any large pieces of chutney. Stir chutney, cherries, lemon juice, salt, and pepper into meat mixture. Bring to boiling; reduce heat. Simmer, covered, for 5 minutes.
3. Spoon meat mixture into taco shells. Top with Feta Cheese Salsa.
FETA CHEESE SALSA: In a medium bowl, combine 1 medium tomato, seeded and finely chopped; ⅓ cup finely chopped cucumber; ¼ cup crumbled reduced-fat feta cheese; ¼ cup finely chopped red onion; ¼ cup finely chopped green sweet pepper; 1 tablespoon olive oil; 1 tablespoon lemon juice; ⅛ teaspoon salt; and ⅛ teaspoon ground black pepper. Stir until combined. Serve with a slotted spoon. Makes about 1½ cups.
PER SERVING: 207 cal., 9 g total fat (3 g sat. fat), 26 mg chol., 274 mg sodium, 21 g carb., 1 g fiber, 8 g pro. Exchanges: 1 starch, 0.5 carb., 1 medium-fat meat, 0.5 fat. Carb choices: 1.5.

Garlic-Chili-Rubbed Lamb

A paste of garlic and spices acts like a marinade as the flavors penetrate the meat during chilling. For a simple side dish, add a few thick slices of tomatoes to the grill rack the last few minutes of grilling. Pictured on page 18.

SERVINGS 4 (2 chops each)
CARB. PER SERVING 3 g

- 4 large cloves garlic, minced
- ½ teaspoon salt
- 1 tablespoon chili powder
- 1 teaspoon ground cumin
- ½ teaspoon sugar
- ½ teaspoon black pepper
- ½ teaspoon dried thyme, crushed
- ¼ teaspoon ground cinnamon
- ¼ teaspoon ground allspice
- 2 to 3 teaspoons olive oil
- 8 lamb rib or loin chops, cut 1 inch thick
  Grilled tomatoes (optional)

1. On a cutting board, using the flat side of a chef's knife, smear together the garlic and salt to form a paste. Transfer garlic paste to a small bowl. Stir in chili powder, cumin, sugar, pepper, thyme, cinnamon, and allspice. Stir in enough olive oil to make a paste. Rub lamb chops all over with the paste. Cover and chill chops for 4 to 24 hours.

2. For a charcoal grill, arrange medium-hot coals around a drip pan. Test for medium heat above the pan. Place chops on grill rack over drip pan. Cover and grill to desired doneness, turning once halfway through grilling. Allow 16 to 18 minutes for medium-rare doneness (145°F) or 18 to 20 minutes for medium doneness (160°F). (For a gas grill, preheat grill. Reduce heat to medium. Adjust for indirect cooking. Grill as above.) If desired, serve with grilled tomatoes.

PER SERVING: 199 cal., 12 g total fat (4 g sat. fat), 64 mg chol., 381 mg sodium, 3 g carb., 1 g fiber, 20 g pro. Exchanges: 3 medium-fat meat. Carb choices: 0.

Oven-Fried Parmesan Chicken

Refrigerated egg product and fat-free milk make this cheese-crusted chicken an ideal dinnertime headliner. It's also great for a potluck—cover and chill the chicken, then transport in an insulated cooler with ice packs.

SERVINGS 12 (1 piece each)
CARB. PER SERVING 6 g

- ½ cup refrigerated or frozen egg product, thawed, or 2 eggs, beaten
- ¼ cup fat-free milk
- ¾ cup grated Parmesan cheese
- ¾ cup fine dry bread crumbs
- 2 teaspoons dried oregano, crushed
- 1 teaspoon paprika
- ¼ teaspoon black pepper
- 5 pounds meaty chicken pieces, skinned (breast halves, thighs, and drumsticks)
- ¼ cup butter, melted
  Snipped fresh oregano (optional)
  Lemon wedges (optional)

1. Preheat oven to 375°F. Grease two large shallow baking pans; set aside. In a small bowl, combine eggs and milk. In a shallow dish, combine Parmesan cheese, bread crumbs, oregano, paprika, and pepper.

2. Dip chicken pieces into egg mixture; coat with crumb mixture. Arrange chicken pieces in prepared baking pans, making sure pieces don't touch. Drizzle chicken pieces with melted butter.

3. Bake, uncovered, for 45 to 55 minutes or until chicken is tender and no longer pink (170°F for breasts; 180°F for thighs and drumsticks). Do not turn chicken pieces during baking. Immediately transfer chicken pieces to a covered container; serve within 1 hour. If desired, sprinkle with fresh oregano and serve with lemon wedges.

PER SERVING: 198 cal., 9 g total fat (4 g sat. fat), 79 mg chol., 363 mg sodium, 6 g carb., 0 g fiber, 23 g pro. Exchanges: 0.5 starch, 3 lean meat. Carb choices: 0.5.

Oven-Fried
Parmesan Chicken

Chicken Breasts
with Herbs

Chicken Breasts with Herbs

The herb mixture used in this recipe is a variation on gremolata, a traditional Italian condiment.

SERVINGS 4 (1 breast half and 2 tablespoons cooking liquid each)

CARB. PER SERVING 1 g

- ⅓ cup chopped Italian (flat-leaf) parsley
- 1 tablespoon chopped fresh oregano
- 1 tablespoon finely shredded lemon peel
- 1 tablespoon finely chopped garlic (about 3 cloves)
- 2 tablespoons butter
- 4 skinless, boneless chicken breast halves
- ¼ cup reduced-sodium chicken broth

1. In a bowl, combine parsley, oregano, lemon peel, and garlic. Set aside. Season chicken with *salt* and *black pepper*.
2. In a large skillet, cook chicken in butter over medium-heat for 6 minutes or until browned, turning once. Transfer chicken to plate. Remove skillet from heat; stir in half of the herb mixture. Return skillet to heat. Add broth; bring to boiling, stirring to scrape up browned bits. Return chicken to skillet; reduce heat. Simmer, covered, about 8 minutes or until chicken is no longer pink. Serve with pan sauce; sprinkle with remaining herb mixture.

PER SERVING: 213 cal., 7 g total fat (4 g sat. fat), 97 mg chol., 154 mg sodium, 1 g carb., 0 g fiber, 33 g pro. Exchanges: 4.5 lean meat. Carb choices: 0.

Middle Eastern Chicken Kabobs

If using wooden skewers, soak them in water for 30 minutes before threading on the chicken and veggies.

SERVINGS 6 (1 kabob, ½ pita, and ¼ cup relish each)

CARB. PER SERVING 25 g

- 1 pound skinless, boneless chicken breast halves, cut into 1-inch pieces
- ¼ cup plain low-fat yogurt
- 1 tablespoon lemon juice
- 1 teaspoon dry mustard
- 1 teaspoon ground cinnamon
- 1 teaspoon curry powder
- ½ teaspoon salt
- ¼ to ½ teaspoon crushed red pepper
- 1 large red sweet pepper, cut into 1-inch pieces
- 1 medium yellow summer squash, halved lengthwise and cut into ½-inch-thick slices

Middle Eastern Chicken Kabobs

- 3 whole wheat pita bread rounds, warmed and cut into wedges
- 1 recipe Tomato Relish (below)

1. Place chicken in a resealable plastic bag set in a shallow dish. For marinade: In a small bowl, combine yogurt, lemon juice, mustard, cinnamon, curry powder, salt, and crushed red pepper. Pour over chicken. Seal bag and turn to coat chicken. Marinate in the refrigerator for 1 to 4 hours.
2. Preheat broiler. On six long wooden or metal skewers, alternately thread chicken, sweet pepper, and squash, leaving a ¼-inch space between pieces.
3. Broil 4 to 5 inches from the heat for 8 to 10 minutes or until chicken is no longer pink, turning once.
4. Serve kabobs with pita bread and Tomato Relish.

TOMATO RELISH: In a medium bowl, combine 2 roma tomatoes, coarsely chopped; ½ cup yellow or red grape tomatoes, halved; 1 teaspoon snipped fresh oregano or ¼ teaspoon dried oregano, crushed; 1 teaspoon snipped fresh thyme or ¼ teaspoon dried thyme, crushed; 1 clove garlic, minced; 1 tablespoon white balsamic or balsamic vinegar; 1 teaspoon honey; ⅛ teaspoon salt; and ⅛ teaspoon black pepper. Cover and chill for up to 4 hours.

PER SERVING: 206 cal., 2 g total fat (1 g sat. fat), 44 mg chol., 464 mg sodium, 25 g carb., 4 g fiber, 22 g pro. Exchanges: 1 vegetable, 1 starch, 2.5 lean meat. Carb choices: 1.5.

Kalamata Lemon Chicken

Save some time by skipping the browning step and directly placing the ingredients in a 2-quart rectangular baking dish. The baking time won't change, but your prep time will be knocked down to nearly nothing. Bear in mind the chicken won't be as pretty.

SERVINGS 4
CARB. PER SERVING 25 g

- 1 to 1¼ pounds skinless, boneless chicken thighs
- 1 tablespoon olive oil
- ⅔ cup dried orzo
- ½ cup drained, pitted kalamata olives
- 1 14-ounce can reduced-sodium chicken broth
- ½ of a lemon, cut into wedges or chunks
- 1 tablespoon lemon juice
- 1 teaspoon dried Greek seasoning
- ¼ teaspoon black pepper
  Hot reduced-sodium chicken broth (optional)
  Fresh snipped oregano (optional)

1. Preheat oven to 400°F. In a 4-quart Dutch oven, brown chicken in hot oil over medium-high heat for 5 minutes, turning once. Stir in orzo, olives, the can of broth, lemon wedges, lemon juice, Greek seasoning, and pepper. Bake, covered, about 35 minutes or until chicken is tender and no longer pink. If desired, serve in shallow bowls with additional broth and top with snipped oregano.

PER SERVING: 304 cal., 10 g total fat (2 g sat. fat), 94 mg chol., 523 mg sodium, 25 g carb., 2 g fiber, 27 g pro. Exchanges: 1.5 starch, 3 lean meat, 1 fat. Carb choices: 1.5.

Kalamata
Lemon Chicken

Chicken Potpie

We made this savory pie more healthful by stir-frying the vegetables using nonstick cooking spray instead of butter or cooking oil and using chicken breast rather than dark meat.

SERVINGS 4 (¾ cup each)
CARB. PER SERVING 38 g

- 1 recipe Oil Pastry (below)
- 1½ cups sliced fresh mushrooms
- ½ cup chopped onion
- 1 12-ounce can evaporated fat-free milk
- 3 tablespoons flour
- ¼ cup water
- 1 teaspoon instant chicken bouillon granules
- ½ teaspoon dried sage, marjoram, or thyme, crushed
- ⅛ teaspoon black pepper
- 1½ cups chopped cooked chicken breast or turkey breast (about 8 ounces)
- 1 cup frozen peas with pearl onions

1. Preheat oven to 425°F. Prepare Oil Pastry; form dough into a ball. On a lightly floured surface, flatten dough with hands. Roll pastry to ⅛-inch thickness. Using 1- to 1½-inch cookie cutters, make desired-shape pastry cutouts (do not reroll scraps). Cover pastry; set aside.
2. Lightly coat an unheated medium saucepan with *nonstick cooking spray.* Preheat over medium heat. Add mushrooms and onion to hot pan; cook and stir about 4 minutes or until the onion is tender.
3. Meanwhile, set aside 1 tablespoon of the evaporated milk. In a small bowl, gradually whisk the remaining evaporated milk into the flour until smooth. Stir milk mixture into mushroom mixture in saucepan. Stir in the water, bouillon granules, sage, and pepper. Cook and stir until thickened and bubbly.
4. Stir in chicken and frozen peas with pearl onions. Transfer mixture to a 9-inch deep-dish pie plate. Arrange pastry cutouts on top of hot chicken mixture. Brush pastry cutouts with the reserved 1 tablespoon evaporated milk.
5. Bake for 20 to 25 minutes or until pastry is golden. Let stand for 10 minutes before serving.

OIL PASTRY: In a medium bowl, stir together ⅔ cup flour and ⅛ teaspoon salt. Add 3 tablespoons cooking oil and 2 tablespoons fat-free milk. Stir lightly with a fork to combine.

PER SERVING: 386 cal., 13 g total fat (2 g sat. fat), 48 mg chol., 450 mg sodium, 38 g carb., 3 g fiber, 28 g pro. Exchanges: 0.5 vegetable, 2 starch, 3 lean meat, 1.5 fat. Carb choices: 2.5.

Chicken-Pineapple Fajitas

Chicken-Pineapple Fajitas

A Mexican favorite gets a Caribbean spin with
citrus fruits and Jamaican jerk seasoing.

SERVINGS 4 (1 fajita each)
CARB. PER SERVING 30 g

- 4 8-inch whole wheat flour tortillas
- 4 1-inch slices peeled fresh pineapple (about half)
- 12 ounces skinless, boneless chicken breast halves
- 2 small red and/or orange sweet peppers, cut into strips
- 2 teaspoons Jamaican jerk seasoning
- ⅛ teaspoon black pepper
- 1 tablespoon canola oil
  Fresh cilantro and lime wedges

1. Preheat oven to 350°F. Wrap tortillas in foil and bake 10 minutes to heat through. Meanwhile, coat a very large nonstick skillet with *nonstick cooking spray;* heat over medium-high heat. Add pineapple slices; cook for 4 to 6 minutes or until browned, turning once. Remove.
2. Cut chicken into strips. Toss chicken strips with sweet peppers, jerk seasoning, and black pepper. Heat oil in skillet over medium-high heat; add chicken and peppers. Cook and stir for 4 to 6 minutes or until chicken is no longer pink. Serve chicken with tortillas, cilantro, and lime.

PER SERVING: 315 cal., 8 g total fat (2 g sat. fat), 49 mg chol., 519 mg sodium, 30 g carb., 13 g fiber, 29 g pro. Exchanges: 0.5 vegetable, 0.5 fruit, 1.5 starch, 3.5 lean meat. Carb choices: 2.

Tarragon Chicken Linguine

Cooking broccoli with the linguine lets you use less pasta overall and save on cleanup at the same time.

SERVINGS 4 (1½ cups each)
CARB. PER SERVING 36 g

- 6 ounces dried linguine or fettuccine
- 2 cups broccoli florets
- ½ cup reduced-sodium chicken broth
- 2 teaspoons cornstarch
- ¼ teaspoon lemon-pepper seasoning or black pepper
- 3 skinless, boneless chicken breast halves, cut into bite-size strips (12 ounces total)
- 2 teaspoons olive oil or canola oil
- 1 tablespoon snipped fresh tarragon or dill or ½ teaspoon dried tarragon or dill, crushed

1. Cook pasta according to package directions, adding broccoli the last 4 minutes. Drain; keep warm.
2. Combine broth, cornstarch, and seasoning; set aside.
3. In a large nonstick skillet, cook chicken in hot oil 4 minutes or until no longer pink, stirring often.
4. Stir cornstarch mixture; add to skillet. Cook and stir until thickened. Stir in tarragon; cook for 2 minutes. Serve over pasta.
PER SERVING: 293 cal., 4 g total fat (1 g sat. fat), 49 mg chol., 153 mg sodium, 36 g carb., 2 g fiber, 27 g pro. Exchanges: 1 vegetable, 2 starch, 2.5 lean meat. Carb choices: 2.5.

Tarragon Chicken Linguine

Turkey Enchilada Casserole

Instead of calorie-laden regular sour cream, the creamy enchilada filling includes only a wisp of light sour cream.

SERVINGS 6 (one 4×2½-inch rectangle each)
CARB. PER SERVING 24 g

- ¾ cup water
- ½ cup chopped onion
- ½ teaspoon instant chicken bouillon granules
- 2 cloves garlic, minced
- ⅛ teaspoon black pepper
- ½ cup light sour cream
- 2 tablespoons nonfat dry milk powder
- 1 tablespoon all-purpose flour
- 1½ cups shredded cooked turkey breast or chicken breast (about 8 ounces)
- 1 8-ounce can no-salt-added tomato sauce
- 1 4-ounce can diced green chile peppers, drained, or 1 or 2 canned jalapeño chile peppers, rinsed, seeded, and finely chopped (see tip, page 32)
- 2 tablespoons snipped fresh cilantro or ½ teaspoon ground coriander
- 4 6-inch corn tortillas, cut into 1-inch-wide strips
- 1 cup canned black beans or kidney beans, rinsed and drained
- ½ cup shredded reduced-fat Monterey Jack cheese (2 ounces)

1. Preheat oven to 350°F. For turkey filling: In a medium saucepan, combine the water, onion, bouillon granules, garlic, and black pepper. Bring to boiling; reduce heat. Cover and simmer about 3 minutes or until onion is tender. Do not drain. In a small bowl, combine sour cream, nonfat dry milk powder, and flour; add to onion mixture. Cook and stir until thickened and bubbly. Remove from heat; stir in turkey. Set filling aside.
2. In another small bowl, combine tomato sauce, chile peppers, and snipped cilantro. Set aside.
3. Coat a 2-quart baking dish with *nonstick cooking spray*. Arrange tortilla strips in the baking dish. Top with turkey. Top with beans. Top with tomato sauce mixture.
4. Bake for 25 to 30 minutes or until heated through. Sprinkle with cheese. Let stand for 5 minutes before serving.
PER SERVING: 212 cal., 5 g total fat (2 g sat. fat), 45 mg chol., 398 mg sodium, 24 g carb., 5 g fiber, 21 g pro. Exchanges: 1.5 starch, 2.5 lean meat. Carb choices: 1.5.

Pineapple-Turkey Kabobs

Rum lends a Caribbean flavor, while lemongrass tastes distinctly Asian. More east than west? You decide! (Or simply dig in and call it delicious.)

SERVINGS 4 (2 kabobs and ½ cup rice each)

CARB. PER SERVING 39 g

Pineapple-Turkey Kabobs

12	ounces turkey breast tenderloin
⅓	cup unsweetened pineapple juice
3	tablespoons rum or unsweetened pineapple juice
1	tablespoon finely chopped lemongrass or 2 teaspoons finely shredded lemon peel
1	tablespoon olive oil
1	medium red onion, cut into thin wedges
2	plums or 1 nectarine, pitted and cut into thick slices
1½	cups fresh or canned pineapple chunks
2	cups hot cooked brown rice
¼	cup thinly sliced sugar snap peas

1. Cut turkey into 1-inch cubes. Place turkey in a resealable plastic bag set in a shallow dish. For marinade: In a small bowl, combine the ⅓ cup pineapple juice, the rum or 3 tablespoons pineapple juice, lemongrass, and oil. Pour over turkey. Seal bag; turn to coat turkey. Marinate in the refrigerator for 4 to 24 hours, turning the bag occasionally.

2. Drain turkey, reserving marinade. In a small saucepan, bring marinade to boiling. Boil gently, uncovered, for 1 minute. Remove from heat. On eight 10- to 12-inch skewers, alternately thread turkey and onion, leaving a ¼-inch space between pieces. Alternately thread plum slices and pineapple chunks onto four more skewers.

3. For a charcoal grill, grill turkey and fruit kabobs on the rack of an uncovered grill directly over medium coals until turkey and onion are tender, turkey is no longer pink, and fruit is heated through, turning once and brushing occasionally with marinade during the last half of grilling. (Allow 12 to 14 minutes for turkey and onion and about 5 minutes for fruit.) (For a gas grill, preheat grill. Reduce heat to medium. Place turkey and fruit kabobs on grill rack over heat. Cover and grill as above.)

4. To serve, toss hot cooked rice with snap peas; serve turkey, onion, and fruit with rice.

PER SERVING: 326 cal., 5 g total fat (1 g sat. fat), 53 mg chol., 41 mg sodium, 39 g carb., 3 g fiber, 24 g pro. Exchanges: 1 fruit, 1.5 starch, 3 lean meat. Carb choices: 2.5.

QUICK TIP

Cook a big batch of brown rice at once. Then spoon 2-cup portions of cooled cooked rice into freezer bags or containers and freeze until needed.

Spaghetti Pie

Making the crust with egg whites gives you all the cooking power of whole eggs without the cholesterol. Using low-fat cottage cheese and lean ground beef for traditional sausage reduces the fat in the filling.

SERVINGS 6 (1 wedge each)

CARB. PER SERVING 23 g

- 4 ounces dried spaghetti
- 2 egg whites, lightly beaten
- ⅓ cup grated Parmesan cheese
- 1 tablespoon olive oil
- 2 egg whites, lightly beaten
- 1 12-ounce container (1¼ cups) low-fat cottage cheese, drained
- 8 ounces uncooked ground turkey breast or lean ground beef
- 1 cup sliced fresh mushrooms
- ½ cup chopped onion
- ½ cup chopped green and/or red sweet pepper
- 2 cloves garlic, minced
- 1 8-ounce can no-salt-added tomato sauce
- 1½ teaspoons dried Italian seasoning, crushed
- ⅛ teaspoon salt
- ½ cup shredded part-skim mozzarella cheese (2 ounces)

1. Preheat oven to 350°F. Coat a 9-inch pie plate with nonstick cooking spray; set aside. For crust: Cook spaghetti according to package directions, except omit the cooking oil and salt. Meanwhile, in a medium bowl, stir together 2 egg whites, the Parmesan cheese, and olive oil. Drain spaghetti well; add to egg white mixture and toss to coat. Press spaghetti mixture evenly into the bottom and up the side of the prepared pie plate; set aside.

2. In a small bowl, stir together 2 egg whites and drained cottage cheese. Spread the cottage cheese mixture over the crust in pie plate; set aside.

3. In a large skillet, cook turkey, mushrooms, onion, sweet pepper, and garlic until meat is browned. Drain off fat. Stir tomato sauce, Italian seasoning, and salt into meat mixture in skillet. Spoon over cottage cheese mixture in crust.

4. Bake, uncovered, about 20 minutes or until heated through. Sprinkle with mozzarella cheese. Bake about 5 minutes more or until cheese melts. Let stand for 15 minutes before serving. Cut into wedges to serve.

PER SERVING: 256 cal., 7 g total fat (3 g sat. fat), 27 mg chol., 479 mg sodium, 23 g carb., 2 g fiber, 26 g pro. Exchanges: 0.5 vegetable, 1.5 starch, 3 lean meat. Carb choices: 1.5.

Catfish & Turkey Sausage Jambalaya

Turkey Italian sausage links are traditionally sold in 1-pound packages. Individually wrap remaining sausage links in freezer wrap and freeze for another use.

SERVINGS 4 (1½ cups each)

CARB. PER SERVING 29 g

- 8 ounces fresh or frozen skinless catfish fillets
- 4 ounces uncooked turkey hot Italian sausage links, cut into ½-inch pieces
- 1 teaspoon olive oil or cooking oil
- ½ cup chopped onion
- ½ cup chopped green sweet pepper
- 1 stalk celery, chopped
- 3 cloves garlic, minced
- 1 14.5-ounce can no-salt-added diced tomatoes, drained
- 1 14-ounce can reduced-sodium chicken broth
- 1½ cups instant brown rice
- 1½ teaspoons paprika
- 1 teaspoon dried oregano, crushed, or 1 tablespoon snipped fresh oregano
- ½ teaspoon dried thyme, crushed, or 1½ teaspoons snipped fresh thyme
- ⅛ to ¼ teaspoon cayenne pepper
- Fresh oregano (optional)

1. Thaw fish, if frozen. Rinse fish; pat dry with paper towels. Cut fish into ¾-inch chunks. Set aside.

2. In a large saucepan, cook sausage pieces in hot oil over medium heat for 3 to 4 minutes or until browned. Add onion, sweet pepper, celery, and garlic; cook, stirring occasionally, about 10 minutes or until vegetables are tender and sausage is no longer pink.

3. Stir in tomatoes, chicken broth, uncooked rice, paprika, dried oregano (if using), dried thyme (if using), and cayenne pepper. Bring to boiling; reduce heat to medium-low. Simmer, covered, for 5 minutes. Stir in catfish pieces, fresh oregano (if using), and fresh thyme (if using); cook about 5 minutes more or until liquid is nearly absorbed and rice is tender. Remove from heat. Cover and let stand for 5 minutes. Using a slotted spoon, spoon mixture into shallow bowls. If desired, garnish with fresh oregano.

PER SERVING: 263 cal., 9 g total fat (2 g sat. fat), 44 mg chol., 548 mg sodium, 29 g carb., 4 g fiber, 18 g pro. Exchanges: 1 vegetable, 1.5 starch, 2 lean meat, 0.5 fat. Carb choices: 2.

Catfish & Turkey Sausage Jambalaya

Parmesan-Crusted Fish

Complete this fish and carrot meal with a handful of mixed greens.

SERVINGS 4 (1 fillet and ¾ cup carrots each)
CARB. PER SERVING 11 g

- 4 skinless cod fillets (1½ pounds total)
- ⅓ cup panko (Japanese-style) bread crumbs
- ¼ cup finely shredded Parmesan cheese
- 1 10-ounce package julienned carrots (3 cups)
- 1 tablespoon butter
- ¾ teaspoon ground ginger

1. Preheat oven to 450°F. Lightly coat a baking sheet with *nonstick cooking spray*. Rinse fish; pat dry. Place fish on baking sheet. Season with *salt* and *black pepper*. In small bowl, stir together crumbs and cheese; sprinkle on fish. Bake, uncovered, for 4 to 6 minutes for each ½-inch thickness of fish or until crumbs are golden and fish flakes easily when tested with a fork.

2. Meanwhile, in a large skillet, bring ½ cup *water* to boiling; add carrots. Reduce heat. Cook, covered, for 5 minutes. Uncover; cook for 2 minutes more. Add butter and ginger; toss to coat. Serve fish with carrots.

PER SERVING: 233 cal., 6 g total fat (3 g sat. fat), 84 mg chol., 407 mg sodium, 11 g carb., 2 g fiber, 34 g pro. Exchanges: 1 vegetable, 0.5 starch, 4 lean meat. Carb choices: 1.0.

Gazpacho Fish Fillets

A package of cooked brown rice makes this fabulous no-fuss fish entrée extra easy.

SERVINGS 4 (one 4-ounce fillet, about ⅓ cup tomato mixture, and ⅓ cup rice each)
CARB. PER SERVING 23 g

- 1 pound fresh or frozen fish fillets (such as orange roughy, cod, or other desired fish that is ½ to ¾ inch thick)
- ½ teaspoon salt

Parmesan-Crusted Fish

Herbed Salmon Loaf
with Creamed Peas

1/8 teaspoon ground black pepper
1 large tomato, chopped
1/4 cup chopped, seeded cucumber
1/4 cup chopped green sweet pepper
1/4 cup chopped celery
2 tablespoons chopped onion
2 tablespoons tomato paste
1 tablespoon snipped fresh thyme or 1 teaspoon dried thyme, crushed
  Fresh thyme sprigs (optional)
1 8.8-ounce pouch cooked whole grain brown rice, prepared according to package directions, or 1 1/2 cups hot cooked brown rice

1. Thaw fish, if frozen. Rinse fish; pat dry with paper towels. Cut fish into serving-size portions if necessary. Sprinkle fish with 1/4 teaspoon of the salt and the 1/8 teaspoon black pepper. Set aside.
2. In a microwave-safe 2-quart casserole or baking dish, stir together tomato, cucumber, sweet pepper, celery, onion, tomato paste, snipped or dried thyme, and the remaining 1/4 teaspoon salt. Cover tightly with lid or plastic wrap. Microwave on high (100% power) for 4 to 6 minutes or until celery is crisp-tender. Transfer tomato mixture to a bowl; cover to keep warm.
3. Arrange fish in the same casserole or baking dish. Turn under any thin portions of fish to make an even thickness. Microwave, covered, on high (100% power) for 3 to 5 minutes or until fish flakes easily when tested with a fork.
4. Divide fish fillets and tomato mixture among four dinner plates. If desired, garnish with thyme sprigs. Serve with rice.

PER SERVING: 197 cal., 3 g total fat (0 g sat. fat), 22 mg chol., 378 mg sodium, 23 g carb., 2 g fiber, 20 g pro. Exchanges: 1 vegetable, 1 starch, 2 lean meat. Carb choices: 1.5.

Herbed Salmon Loaf with Creamed Peas

This salmon-and-barley loaf topped with low-fat creamed peas is a healthful makeover of an old classic.
SERVINGS 8 (2 thin slices salmon loaf and 2 tablespoons peas each)
CARB. PER SERVING 13 g

2 14- to 15-ounce cans salmon, drained
1 cup cooked barley*
1 stalk celery, finely chopped
1 small onion, finely chopped

1/4 cup fine dry bread crumbs
2 tablespoons snipped fresh parsley or 2 teaspoons dried parsley flakes
2 tablespoons lemon juice
1 tablespoon snipped fresh dill or 1 teaspoon dried dill
4 egg whites, 1/2 cup refrigerated or frozen egg product, thawed, or 2 eggs, lightly beaten
1 recipe Creamed Peas (below)
  Fresh dill sprigs (optional)

1. Preheat oven to 350°F. Remove skin and bones from salmon. Flake salmon. Combine salmon, barley, celery, onion, bread crumbs, parsley, lemon juice, snipped or dried dill, and 1/4 teaspoon *black pepper*. Stir in egg whites.
2. Lightly coat an 8×4×2-inch loaf pan with *nonstick cooking spray*. Press salmon mixture into pan. Bake about 1 hour or until an instant-read thermometer inserted into center of loaf registers 160°F. Cover and let stand for 10 minutes.
3. To serve, carefully invert pan to remove loaf. Invert loaf again and transfer to a serving platter. Cut into slices. Serve warm with Creamed Peas. If desired, garnish with fresh dill sprigs.

CREAMED PEAS: In a small saucepan, stir together 1 cup fat-free milk, 2 1/2 teaspoons cornstarch, 1/4 teaspoon salt, and dash black pepper. Cook and stir until thickened and bubbly. Cook and stir for 2 minutes more. Stir in 1/2 cup cooked fresh or frozen peas and 1/8 teaspoon finely shredded lemon peel. Heat through. Makes about 1 cup.

*TEST KITCHEN TIP: To make 1 cup cooked barley, in a small saucepan, combine 3/4 cup water and 1/3 cup uncooked quick-cooking barley. Bring to boiling; reduce heat. Simmer, covered, for 10 to 12 minutes or until barley is tender. Drain if necessary.

PER SERVING: 206 cal., 5 g total fat (1 g sat. fat), 82 mg chol., 561 mg sodium, 13 g carb., 2 g fiber, 27 g pro. Exchanges: 1 starch, 3 lean meat. Carb choices: 1.

Grilled Lemon-Herb Halibut

Fresh oregano, garlic, and lemon-pepper seasoning bring out the best in the delicate flavor of halibut.

SERVINGS 2 (1 halibut steak each)
CARB. PER SERVING 3 g

- 2 6-ounce fresh or frozen halibut steaks, cut 1 inch thick
- 2 tablespoons lemon juice
- 1 tablespoon snipped fresh oregano or thyme or ½ teaspoon dried oregano or thyme, crushed
- 2 teaspoons olive oil
- 2 cloves garlic, minced
- 1 teaspoon lemon-pepper seasoning
   Fresh oregano or thyme leaves (optional)
   Lemon wedges (optional)

1. Thaw fish, if frozen. Rinse fish; pat dry with paper towels. Place fish in a resealable plastic bag set in a shallow dish. For marinade: In a small bowl, combine lemon juice, snipped or crushed oregano or thyme, oil, garlic, and lemon-pepper seasoning. Pour over fish; turn to coat. Marinate in refrigerator for at least 30 minutes or up to 1½ hours, turning bag occasionally.
2. Preheat broiler. Drain fish, reserving marinade. Place fish on the greased unheated rack of a broiler pan. Broil 4 inches from the heat for 8 to 12 minutes or until fish flakes easily when tested with a fork, turning once and brushing once with reserved marinade halfway through broiling. Discard any remaining marinade. If desired, garnish with fresh oregano or thyme leaves. If desired, serve with lemon wedges.

PER SERVING: 238 cal., 8 g total fat (1 g sat. fat), 54 mg chol., 636 mg sodium, 3 g carb., 0 g fiber, 36 g pro. Exchanges: 5 lean meat. Carb choices: 0.

Mexican-Style Shrimp Pizza

Flour tortillas make easy low-calorie, low-fat crusts for these south-of-the-border sensations.

SERVINGS 2 (1 pizza each)
CARB. PER SERVING 22 g

- 2 8-inch flour tortillas
- 1 teaspoon olive oil
- 1 cup thin bite-size red and/or yellow sweet pepper strips
- ⅓ cup thinly sliced green onions
- ½ of a medium fresh jalapeño chile pepper, seeded and thinly sliced* (optional)
- 1 tablespoon water
- 2 to 3 tablespoons purchased green salsa
- 4 ounces peeled and deveined cooked medium shrimp
- ⅓ cup shredded Monterey Jack cheese
- 1 tablespoon snipped fresh cilantro

1. Preheat oven to 400°F. Brush both sides of each tortilla with oil; place on an ungreased baking sheet. Bake about 10 minutes or until crisp, turning once.
2. Meanwhile, coat an unheated medium nonstick skillet with *nonstick cooking spray*. Preheat skillet over medium heat. Add sweet pepper, green onions, and, if desired, chile pepper. Cook about 5 minutes or until nearly crisp-tender, stirring occasionally. Add the water; cover and cook for 2 minutes more. Spread each tortilla with about 1 tablespoon of the green salsa. Top with cooked vegetable mixture and shrimp. Sprinkle with cheese. Bake about 3 minutes or until cheese melts and shrimp is heated through. Sprinkle with cilantro.
***TEST KITCHEN TIP:** Because chile peppers contain volatile oils that can burn your skin and eyes, avoid direct contact with them as much as possible. When working with chile peppers, wear plastic or rubber gloves. If your bare hands do touch the peppers, wash your hands and nails well with soap and warm water.

PER SERVING: 265 cal., 11 g total fat (5 g sat. fat), 127 mg chol., 407 mg sodium, 22 g carb., 3 g fiber, 20 g pro. Exchanges: 0.5 vegetable, 1.5 starch, 1.5 lean meat, 0.5 high-fat meat. Carb choices: 1.5.

Mexican-Style
Shrimp Pizza

Shrimp and Vegetable
Pasta Toss

recipe on page 35

Grilled Lemon-
Herb Halibut

Make It a Meal

Turn broiled, baked, or grilled meat
or fish into a complete meal with
one of these simple dishes to serve
alongside.

1. **Drizzle cooked carrot coins**
   with a bit of melted butter
   and sprinkle with a snipped
   fresh dill.

2. **Sprinkle roasted sweet
   potato wedges** with a few
   toasted slivered almonds.

3. **Dust steamed green beans
   or broccoli** with a few
   shreds of fresh Parmesan
   cheese and lemon peel.

4. **Make a pilaf** of cooked
   brown rice and assorted
   chopped fresh vegetables.

5. **Serve slices of fresh
   tomato** with a sprinkling of
   snipped fresh basil.

6. **Top wedges of iceberg
   lettuce** with a little creamy
   salad dressing.

7. **Make a salad of spinach,**
   thin apple slices, and a little
   poppy seed dressing.

Poached Halibut and Peppers

Capers come packed in a salty brine. Measure the capers into a small fine-mesh sieve and hold it under cold running water to wash away the brine.

SERVINGS 4 (1 fillet and $1/3$ cup liquid mixture each)
CARB. PER SERVING 9 g

$1\frac{1}{2}$ cups dry white wine (Sauvignon Blanc or Pinot Grigio) or reduced-sodium chicken broth
1 cup water
2 medium yellow and/or red sweet peppers, chopped ($1\frac{1}{2}$ cups)
3 tablespoons drained capers
4 cloves garlic, minced
$\frac{1}{4}$ to $\frac{1}{2}$ teaspoon crushed red pepper
4 halibut fillets or 4 cod or other whitefish fillets (1 to $1\frac{1}{2}$ pounds total)
$\frac{1}{4}$ teaspoon salt
$\frac{1}{8}$ teaspoon black pepper
1 tablespoon olive oil
Coarsely chopped fresh basil

1. In a large skillet, combine wine, water, sweet peppers, capers, garlic, and crushed red pepper. Bring to boiling; reduce heat. Simmer, uncovered, for 7 minutes, stirring occasionally.

2. Place fish in a single layer in the liquid in skillet. Season fish with salt and pepper. Spoon liquid over fish. Return to simmer. Cook, covered, for 4 to 6 minutes per $1/2$-inch thickness of fish or until fish flakes easily when tested with a fork. Remove fish to a serving platter and pour cooking liquid into a small serving pitcher. Drizzle cooked fish with olive oil and a little of the cooking liquid. Sprinkle with basil. Serve with remaining liquid mixture.

PER SERVING: 260 cal., 6 g total fat (1 g sat. fat), 36 mg chol., 402 mg sodium, 9 g carb., 1 g fiber, 25 g pro. Exchanges: 0.5 vegetable, 0.5 carb., 3.5 lean meat, 1 fat. Carb choices: 0.5.

Poached Halibut and Peppers

Three-Cheese Manicotti

Shrimp and Vegetable Pasta Toss

A can of tomato sauce with herbs gives this light sauce a hint of marinara. Pictured on page 33.

SERVINGS 4 (about 1½ cups each)

CARB. PER SERVING 31 g

- 12 ounces fresh or frozen medium shrimp, peeled and deveined
- 4 ounces dried multigrain angel hair pasta
- 1 large onion, halved and thinly sliced
- 2 tablespoons butter
- ¼ to ½ teaspoon crushed red pepper
- 1 8-ounce can tomato sauce with basil, garlic, and oregano
- 1 medium yellow summer squash or zucchini, halved lengthwise and thinly sliced
- ⅛ teaspoon salt
- 4 cups packaged baby spinach
- 1 cup cherry tomatoes, halved
- 2 tablespoons finely shredded Parmesan cheese

1. Thaw shrimp, if frozen. Cook pasta according to package directions; drain.

2. Meanwhile, in an extra large skillet, cook onion in butter until tender. Add shrimp and crushed red pepper; cook and stir for 1 minute. Add tomato sauce, squash, and salt. Bring to boiling; reduce heat. Simmer, covered, for 5 minutes.

3. Stir drained pasta, spinach, and cherry tomatoes into skillet. Toss gently over medium heat until heated through. Sprinkle with Parmesan cheese.

PER SERVING: 279 cal., 8 g total fat (4 g sat. fat), 114 mg chol., 588 mg sodium, 31 g carb., 5 g fiber, 21 g pro. Exchanges: 2 vegetable, 1.5 starch, 2 lean meat. Carb choices: 2.

Three-Cheese Manicotti

Rinse the cooked manicotti shells in cold water to keep them from sticking together while you stuff them with filling.

SERVINGS 10 (2 filled shells each)

CARB. PER SERVING 37 g

- 20 dried manicotti shells
- 2½ cups low-fat ricotta cheese (24 ounces)
- 2 cups shredded part-skim mozzarella cheese (8 ounces)
- ½ cup refrigerated or frozen egg product, thawed, or 2 eggs
- ⅓ cup grated Romano or Asiago cheese
- ¼ cup snipped fresh parsley
- ¼ teaspoon black pepper
- 4 cups purchased light tomato basil pasta sauce
  Snipped fresh parsley (optional)

1. Cook manicotti shells according to package directions. Set aside. For filling: In a large bowl, combine ricotta cheese, 1 cup of the mozzarella cheese, the eggs, Romano cheese, the ¼ cup parsley, and the pepper.

2. Preheat oven to 350°F. Spread 1 cup of the pasta sauce in the bottom of a 3-quart rectangular baking dish. Spoon about 3 tablespoons of the filling into each cooked shell. Arrange in prepared baking dish. Spoon remaining pasta sauce evenly over filled shells in baking dish.

3. Bake, uncovered, for 35 to 40 minutes or until heated through. Sprinkle with the remaining 1 cup mozzarella cheese. Bake about 5 minutes more or until cheese melts. Let stand on a wire rack for 10 minutes before serving. If desired, sprinkle with additional parsley.

PER SERVING: 293 cal., 8 g total fat (4 g sat. fat), 36 mg chol., 640 mg sodium, 37 g carb., 3 g fiber, 20 g pro. Exchanges: 0.5 vegetable, 2 starch, 2 medium-fat meat. Carb choices: 2.5.

Asparagus-Leek Risotto

To save time, while the asparagus is roasting, cook the leeks, brown the rice, and heat the broth to simmering.

SERVINGS 4 (about ¾ cup risotto and 1 or 2 asparagus spears each)

CARB. PER SERVING 36 g

- 12 ounces fresh asparagus spears, trimmed
- 2 tablespoons olive oil
- 1½ cups sliced leeks
- 1 cup Arborio rice
- 3 cups reduced-sodium chicken broth
- ⅓ cup freshly grated Parmesan cheese
- 2 tablespoons snipped fresh parsley
- ½ teaspoon finely shredded lemon peel
- 1 tablespoon lemon juice
- ¼ teaspoon freshly ground coarse black pepper
  Lemon slices and/or lemon peel

1. Preheat oven to 450°F. Place asparagus in single layer on a baking sheet. Brush with 1 tablespoon of the olive oil; lightly sprinkle with *salt* and *black pepper*. Roast about 10 minutes or until crisp-tender. Cool slightly. Cut two-thirds of the asparagus into 2-inch pieces; set aside all asparagus.

2. Meanwhile, in a large saucepan, cook leeks in remaining olive oil until tender. Stir in uncooked rice. Cook and stir over medium heat about 5 minutes or until rice begins to turn golden brown.

3. In another saucepan, bring broth to boiling. Reduce heat and simmer. Carefully stir 1 cup of hot broth into rice mixture. Cook, stirring frequently, over medium heat until liquid is absorbed. Then add ½ cup broth at a time, stirring frequently until broth is absorbed before adding more broth (about 22 minutes).

4. Stir in any remaining broth. Cook and stir just until rice is tender and creamy.

5. Stir in asparagus pieces, cheese, parsley, lemon peel, lemon juice, and coarse black pepper. Top with asparagus spears and lemon slices and/or lemon peel.

PER SERVING: 256 cal., 9 g total fat (2 g sat. fat), 6 mg chol., 683 mg sodium, 36 g carb., 3 g fiber, 10 g pro. Exchanges: 1 vegetable, 2 starch, 1 lean meat, 2.5 fat. Carb choices: 2.5.

Penne with Walnuts and Peppers

Just a sprinkling of walnuts lends crunch and flavor to this pasta dish without adding a lot of fat or calories.

SERVINGS 4 (1⅔ cups each) main dish or 10 (¾ cup each) side dish

CARB. PER SERVING 40 g

- 6 ounces dried whole wheat or multigrain penne or rotelle pasta
- 1 tablespoon olive oil
- ¼ cup coarsely chopped walnuts
- 4 large cloves garlic, thinly sliced
- 2 medium green, red, and/or yellow sweet peppers, cut lengthwise into bite-size strips
- 1 small red onion, cut into thin wedges
- 1 cup halved red and/or yellow cherry and/or grape tomatoes
- ¼ cup snipped fresh parsley
- 2 teaspoons snipped fresh rosemary or ½ teaspoon dried rosemary, crushed
- ¼ teaspoon coarsely ground black pepper
- 2 tablespoons grated Parmesan cheese (optional)

Asparagus-Leek Risotto

Roasted Pepper and Artichoke Pizza

▶ QUICK TIP

For a crispier crust, bake this Mediterranean pie on a baking stone according to the manufacturer's directions.

Roasted Pepper and Artichoke Pizza

No leftover cooked chicken? Look for frozen chopped cooked chicken in your supermarket's freezer case.

SERVINGS 8
CARB. PER SERVING 20 g

1	6- to 6½-ounce package pizza crust mix
1	teaspoon dried oregano or basil, crushed
½	cup pizza sauce
1	cup coarsely chopped or shredded cooked chicken breast (about 5 ounces)
1	6-ounce jar marinated artichoke hearts, drained and coarsely chopped
1	cup bottled roasted red and/or yellow sweet peppers, cut into strips
¼	cup sliced green onions or chopped red onion
½	cup shredded part-skim mozzarella cheese (2 ounces)
4	ounces semisoft goat cheese (chèvre), crumbled

1. Cook pasta according to package directions. Drain and set aside.

2. Meanwhile, in a large skillet, heat oil over medium heat. Add walnuts and garlic. Cook about 2 minutes or until light brown, stirring frequently. Add sweet peppers and red onion. Cook for 5 to 7 minutes or until vegetables are crisp-tender, stirring frequently. Add tomatoes; cook and stir until heated through. Stir in parsley, rosemary, and black pepper.

3. To serve, put pasta in a large shallow bowl. Top with walnut-pepper mixture; toss gently to coat. If desired, sprinkle with Parmesan cheese.

PER MAIN-DISH SERVING: 268 cal., 10 g total fat (1 g sat. fat), 0 mg chol., 7 mg sodium, 40 g carb., 5 g fiber, 9 g pro. Exchanges: 1 vegetable, 2 starch, 1.5 fat. Carb choices: 2.5.

1. Preheat oven to 425°F. Grease a large baking sheet; set aside. Prepare pizza crust according to package directions, except stir oregano into dry mix. With floured hands, pat dough into a 15×10-inch rectangle on prepared baking sheet, building up edges slightly (crust will be thin). Bake for 7 minutes.

2. Spread pizza sauce evenly over crust. Top with chicken, artichokes, roasted peppers, and green onions. Top with mozzarella cheese and goat cheese.

3. Bake for 13 to 15 minutes more or until edges of crust are golden brown.

PER SERVING: 203 cal., 9 g total fat (3 g sat. fat), 27 mg chol., 410 mg sodium, 20 g carb., 1 g fiber, 12 g pro. Exchanges: 0.5 vegetable, 1 starch, 1 medium-fat meat, 1 fat. Carb choices: 1.5.

fresh salad
meals

Remember when a salad of bland iceberg lettuce and a few shreds of carrot was considered diet food? No more. Try these one-dish delights featuring assortments of greens, lean meats, vibrant veggies, and plenty of other healthful ingredients.

Beef and Fruit Salad

This salad boasts the flavors of Japanese cuisine. A mix of teriyaki sauce, sesame oil, and pepper sauce does twice the work as both marinade and dressing.

SERVINGS 4 (3 ounces meat and 1½ cups cabbage-lettuce-fruit mixture each)
CARB. PER SERVING 17 g

12 ounces boneless beef top sirloin steak, cut 1 inch thick
⅓ cup bottled reduced-sodium teriyaki sauce or reduced-sodium soy sauce
¼ cup lemon juice
¼ cup water
2 teaspoons toasted sesame oil
⅛ teaspoon bottled hot pepper sauce
3 cups shredded napa cabbage
1 cup torn or shredded fresh sorrel or fresh spinach
2 cups fresh fruit (such as sliced kiwifruits, plums, or nectarines; halved strawberries or seedless grapes; raspberries; and/or blueberries)

1. Trim fat from steak. Place steak in a resealable plastic bag set in a shallow dish. For marinade: In a small bowl, combine teriyaki sauce or soy sauce, lemon juice, the water, oil, and hot pepper sauce; reserve ⅓ cup for dressing. Pour remaining marinade over steak; seal bag. Marinate in refrigerator for at least 2 hours or up to 8 hours, turning bag occasionally.
2. Preheat broiler. Drain steak, reserving marinade. Place steak on the unheated rack of a broiler pan. Broil 3 to 4 inches from heat to desired doneness, turning once and brushing occasionally with marinade from bag up to the last 5 minutes of broiling time. Allow 15 to 17 minutes for medium-rare doneness (145°F) or 20 to 22 minutes for medium doneness (160°F). Discard any remaining marinade.
3. To serve, divide cabbage and sorrel or spinach among four dinner plates. Thinly slice steak diagonally. Arrange steak and fruit on top of greens. Drizzle with the reserved dressing.
PER SERVING: 207 cal., 7 g total fat (2 g sat. fat), 52 mg chol., 380 mg sodium, 17 g carb., 3 g fiber, 21 g pro. Exchanges: 1 vegetable, 1 fruit, 2.5 medium-fat meat. Carb choices: 1.

▶ QUICK TIP

Bagged salad greens are washed and ready to use, but you should still give them a quick rinse. To dry, whirl the greens in a salad spinner or pat with paper towels.

Blackberry Salad
with Pork

Blackberry Salad with Pork

If you wish, toast more pine nuts than needed for this fab fruit salad. Once cooled, place the nuts in a freezer bag or container and freeze for another salad.

SERVINGS 4 (2 cups each)

CARB. PER SERVING 27 g

- 1 10- to 12-ounce pork tenderloin
- ¼ teaspoon salt
- ¼ teaspoon black pepper
- ½ cup blackberries and/or raspberries
- ¼ cup lemon juice
- 3 tablespoons olive oil
- 3 tablespoons honey
- 6 cups packaged mixed baby greens (spring mix)
- 2 cups blackberries and/or raspberries
- 1 cup grape tomatoes, halved
- 2 tablespoons pine nuts, toasted* (optional)

1. Preheat oven to 425°F. Place pork on a rack in a shallow roasting pan. Sprinkle with ⅛ teaspoon each salt and pepper. Roast, uncovered, for 25 to 35 minutes or until an instant-read thermometer inserted in center registers 155°F. Remove roast from oven. Cover roast with foil and let stand for 5 minutes or until thermometer registers 160°F. Cool slightly. Thinly slice pork.

2. For blackberry vinaigrette: In a blender or food processor, combine the ½ cup blackberries, the lemon juice, oil, honey, and ⅛ teaspoon each salt and pepper. Cover and blend or process until smooth. Strain dressing through a sieve; discard seeds.

3. To serve, place greens in salad bowls or on individual plates; top with the 2 cups blackberries, the tomatoes, pine nuts (if using), and pork slices. Drizzle with dressing. Serve immediately.

***TEST KITCHEN TIP:** To toast pine nuts, place pine nuts in a shallow baking pan. Bake in a 350°F oven for 5 to 7 minutes, shaking pan once or twice. Watch closely so nuts don't burn.

PER SERVING: 277 cal., 12 g total fat (2 g sat. fat), 46 mg chol., 198 mg sodium, 27 g carb., 6 g fiber, 18 g pro. Exchanges: 2 vegetable, 1 fruit, 2 lean meat, 1.5 fat. Carb choices: 2.

Sesame and Ginger Chicken Salad

For casual fare, push your fork aside and eat this popular appetizer like salad out of hand. Roll the lettuce leaves around the chicken mixture and dip each bite in dressing.

SERVINGS 4 (about ¾ cup chicken-carrot mixture and about 3 lettuce leaves each)
CARB. PER SERVING 12 g

1 pound skinless, boneless chicken breast, cut into bite-size strips
Salt
Black pepper
¼ cup bottled light Asian-style dressing with sesame and ginger
2 cups packaged julienned carrots
⅛ teaspoon crushed red pepper
1 head Bibb or Boston lettuce, leaves separated
¼ cup honey-roasted peanuts, chopped
Lime wedges

1. Sprinkle chicken lightly with salt and black pepper. Lightly coat a large skillet with *nonstick cooking spray;* heat over medium-high heat. Add chicken; cook and stir about 3 minutes or until browned. Add 1 tablespoon of the dressing and the carrots to skillet; cook and stir for 2 to 3 minutes more or until carrots are crisp-tender and chicken is no longer pink. Stir in red pepper.
2. To serve, stack lettuce leaves on plates. Top with chicken-carrot mixture. Sprinkle with chopped nuts. Serve with remaining dressing and lime wedges.
PER SERVING: 231 cal., 7 g total fat (1 g sat. fat), 66 mg chol., 436 mg sodium, 12 g carb., 3 g fiber, 29 g pro. Exchanges: 1.5 vegetable, 4 lean meat, 0.5 fat. Carb choices: 1.

Chicken and Spinach Salad
with Avocado Dressing

Superfoods Salad

Chicken and Spinach Salad with Avocado Dressing

Bursting with vegetables, this one-dish favorite provides essential vitamins and minerals.

SERVINGS 8 (about 1⅔ cups each)
CARB. PER SERVING 9 g

1	6-ounce package fresh baby spinach (about 6 cups)
4	cups chopped or shredded cooked chicken
1	medium cucumber, halved lengthwise, seeded, and sliced
1	cup cherry tomatoes, halved
2	medium red, yellow, and/or green sweet peppers, cut into thin strips
1	small red onion, thinly sliced
¼	cup snipped fresh cilantro
1	large ripe avocado, halved, seeded, peeled, and cut up
2	cloves garlic, minced
2	teaspoons finely shredded lime peel
2	tablespoons lime juice
⅔	cup light sour cream
2	tablespoons snipped fresh cilantro
½	teaspoon salt
⅛	teaspoon black pepper
	Bottled hot pepper sauce

1. In a large serving bowl, toss together spinach, chicken, cucumber, cherry tomatoes, sweet peppers, half of the red onion, and the ¼ cup cilantro. Set aside.
2. For dressing: In a food processor,* combine avocado, remaining red onion, garlic, and lime juice. Cover and process until mixture is smooth. Stir in lime peel, sour cream, the 2 tablespoons cilantro, salt, and black pepper. Season to taste with bottled hot pepper sauce. If desired, stir in 1 to 2 tablespoons *water* to make dressing desired consistency.
3. To serve, spoon dressing over spinach mixture. Toss gently to combine.
***TEST KITCHEN TIP:** If you don't have a food processor, mash avocado with a fork or potato masher. Finely chop the onion. Stir ingredients together.
PER SERVING: 214 cal., 10 g total fat (3 g sat. fat), 68 mg chol., 241 mg sodium, 9 g carb., 3 g fiber, 23 g pro. Exchanges: 1.5 vegetable, 3 lean meat, 1 fat. Carb choices: 0.5.

Superfoods Salad

Spinach, strawberries, blueberries, and walnuts are labeled superfoods because they're loaded with antioxidants, touted as contributing to good health.

SERVINGS 4 (about 2 cups each)
CARB. PER SERVING 22 g

⅓	cup raspberry vinegar
2	tablespoons snipped fresh mint
2	tablespoons honey
1	tablespoon canola oil
¼	teaspoon salt
4	cups packaged fresh baby spinach leaves
2	cups chopped cooked chicken breast
2	cups fresh strawberries, hulled and sliced
½	cup fresh blueberries
¼	cup walnuts, toasted and coarsely chopped
1	ounce semisoft goat cheese (chévre), crumbled
½	teaspoon freshly ground black pepper

1. For vinaigrette: In a screw-top jar, combine vinegar, mint, honey, oil, and salt. Cover and shake well.
2. In a large bowl, toss together spinach, chicken, strawberries, blueberries, walnuts, and goat cheese. Transfer to salad plates. Drizzle with vinaigrette and sprinkle with pepper.
PER SERVING: 303 cal., 13 g total fat (2 g sat. fat), 63 mg chol., 249 mg sodium, 22 g carb., 3 g fiber, 26 g pro. Exchanges: 1 vegetable, 0.5 fruit, 0.5 carb., 3.5 lean meat, 1 fat. Carb choices: 1.5.

Southwest Chicken Salad with Mango Salsa

Along with mangoes and blueberries comes an ample amount of dietary fiber. And lucky for you, along with fiber comes a longer feeling of fullness.

SERVINGS 6 (about 2 cups each)

CARB. PER SERVING 31 g

- 2 tablespoons chili powder
- 1 teaspoon salt
- 1 teaspoon garlic powder
- 1 teaspoon ground cumin
- ½ teaspoon black pepper
- ¼ teaspoon cayenne pepper
- 3 tablespoons olive oil or canola oil
- 6 skinless, boneless chicken breast halves
- 8 cups torn mixed greens
- 1 recipe Mango Salsa (below)
- Fresh mint sprigs (optional)

1. In a small bowl, stir together chili powder, salt, garlic powder, cumin, black pepper, and cayenne pepper. Stir in oil. Brush mixture on both sides of chicken breasts. Place in a shallow dish; cover and chill for 30 minutes.

2. For a charcoal grill, place chicken on the grill rack directly over medium coals. Grill, uncovered, for 12 to 15 minutes or until chicken is longer pink (170°F), turning once halfway through grilling. (For a gas grill, preheat grill. Reduce heat to medium. Place chicken on grill rack over heat. Grill as above.)

3. Slice chicken into bite-size strips; toss with greens and Mango Salsa. If desired, garnish with fresh mint sprigs.

MANGO SALSA: In a medium bowl, combine 3 medium mangoes, seeded, peeled, and cubed; 1 cup blueberries; ⅓ cup finely chopped red onion; 3 tablespoons lime juice; 2 tablespoons snipped fresh mint; 2 tablespoons honey; and ¼ teaspoon crushed red pepper.

PER SERVING: 335 cal., 10 g total fat (2 g sat. fat), 77 mg chol., 497 mg sodium, 31 g carb., 5 g fiber, 33 g pro. Exchanges: 1.5 vegetable, 1 fruit, 0.5 carb., 4 lean meat, 0.5 fat. Carb choices: 2.

Curried Chicken Salad

If you're a cashew lover, you can substitute unsalted cashews for the sliced almonds.

SERVINGS 4 (1 cup chicken mixture and 2 lettuce leaves each)

CARB. PER SERVING 24 g

- 2 skinless, boneless chicken breast halves (about 8 ounces total)
- Nonstick cooking spray
- Onion powder
- Garlic powder
- 1 Gala or Fuji apple, cored and chopped
- ½ cup chopped green onions
- ½ cup chopped celery
- ⅓ cup unpacked seedless golden raisins
- ¼ cup sliced almonds
- 1 recipe Curried Salad Dressing (below)
- 8 Boston or Bibb lettuce leaves
- Sliced almonds (optional)

1. Coat chicken with cooking spray. Heat a medium nonstick skillet over medium heat. Sprinkle chicken with onion powder and garlic powder. Cook for 4 to 5 minutes on each side or until no longer pink. Cool slightly; cut chicken into bite-size pieces.

2. In a medium bowl, combine apple, green onions, and celery. Add the cooked chicken, raisins, and the ¼ cup almonds. Spoon Curried Salad Dressing over the salad and stir to coat. Cover and chill for 1 hour.

3. To serve, spoon ½ cup salad into each lettuce leaf and, if desired, sprinkle with additional almonds.

CURRIED SALAD DRESSING: In a small bowl, combine ½ cup light sour cream, 1 to 2 teaspoons curry powder, 1 teaspoon honey, ½ teaspoon ground ginger, and dash cayenne pepper. Stir until smooth. Chill until ready to use.

PER SERVING: 209 cal., 6 g total fat (2 g sat. fat), 41 mg chol., 69 mg sodium, 24 g carb., 3 g fiber, 16 g pro. Exchanges: 1 vegetable, 1 fruit, 2 lean meat, 0.5 fat. Carb choices: 1.5.

Turkey-Broccoli Salad with Grapes
recipe on page 46

Southwest Chicken
Salad with Mango Salsa

Curried Chicken Salad

Toss-Ins

Update your standard dinner salad with ingredients that lend healthful fats, fiber, and antioxidants. Check out this list for smart additions to your salad.

1. **Beans:** Black beans, pinto beans, chickpeas—any type of bean will do. Keep several cans on hand, and rinse and drain the beans when ready to use.

2. **Nuts:** Toast whole walnuts, pecans, and almonds, then roughly chop the nuts and use just a tablespoon for flavor and crunch.

3. **Dried fruit:** A tablespoon of dried cranberries, cherries, or other dried fruit will boost the flavor in your salad.

4. **Fresh fruit:** Chopped apple, peach, pear, pineapple, or other fruit adds color, texture, and sweetness.

until bacon is crisp. Carefully remove the pie plate from the microwave. Set aside cooked bacon slices aside to cool. Meanwhile, cook the peas, covered, in a small amount of boiling salted water for 2 to 4 minutes or until crisp-tender; drain. Crumble one bacon slice; set aside. Break remaining bacon slices into 1-inch pieces.

2. For dressing: In a small bowl, combine mayonnaise, mustard, vinegar, and dill; season to taste with pepper. Stir in crumbled bacon.

3. Divide romaine among bowls. Top with sugar snap peas, turkey, and bacon. Serve with dressing.

PER SERVING: 212 cal., 10 g total fat (2 g sat. fat), 73 mg chol., 484 mg sodium, 6 g carb., 2 g fiber, 21 g pro. Exchanges: 1.5 vegetable, 2.5 lean meat, 1.5 fat. Carb choices: 0.5.

Turkey-Broccoli Salad with Grapes

Rich in vitamins C, A, and K, broccoli slaw mix makes this salad nutritious as well as super easy to prepare. Pictured on page 45.

SERVINGS 6 (1½ cups each)

CARB. PER SERVING 14 g or 13 g

⅓ cup white balsamic vinegar
2 tablespoons olive oil
2 teaspoons sugar*
1 12-ounce package shredded broccoli (broccoli slaw mix)
1 pound cooked turkey breast, shredded
1½ cups seedless red grapes, halved
1 cup coarsely shredded carrots
¼ cup sliced or slivered almonds, toasted, or sunflower kernels
⅛ teaspoon coarsely ground black pepper

1. For vinaigrette: In a screw-top jar, combine vinegar, oil, sugar, and ⅛ teaspoon salt. Cover and shake well.

2. In a very large bowl, combine shredded broccoli, turkey, grapes, and carrots. Add dressing; toss to coat. Serve immediately or cover and chill for up to 24 hours. Sprinkle with almonds and pepper just before serving.

***SUGAR SUBSTITUTES:** Choose from Splenda granular, Equal Spoonful or packets, or Sweet'N Low bulk or packets. Follow package directions to use product amount equivalent to 2 teaspoons sugar.

PER SERVING: 226 cal., 7 g total fat (1 g sat. fat), 63 mg chol., 120 mg sodium, 14 g carb., 3 g fiber, 25 g pro. Exchanges: 1 vegetable, 0.5 fruit, 3 lean meat, 1 fat. Carb choices: 1.

PER SERVING WITH SUBSTITUTE: Same as above, except 221 cal., 13 g carb.

Turkey and Sugar Snap Pea Salad

Serve the creamy dressing on the side. You'll save calories and fat by lightly dipping each bite in dressing rather than tossing it with the salad.

SERVINGS 4

CARB. PER SERVING 6 g

5 slices turkey bacon
2 cups sugar snap peas
⅓ cup light mayonnaise or salad dressing
1 tablespoon Dijon-style mustard
1 tablespoon cider vinegar
1 tablespoon snipped fresh dill
Black pepper
1 small head romaine, coarsely chopped or torn
8 ounces cooked turkey breast, cut into chunks

1. Line a 9-inch microwave-safe pie plate with paper towels. Arrange bacon slices in a single layer on top of the paper towels. Cover with additional paper towels. Microwave on 100% power (high) for 4 to 5 minutes or

Thai Tuna Toss

Shred leftover cabbage and stir it into a kettle of vegetable soup, toss it into a green salad, or add it to a stir-fry.

SERVINGS 4 (2 cups each)

CARB. PER SERVING 14 g

- 6 cups shredded napa or Chinese cabbage
- 12 ounces cooked tuna, broken into chunks, or two 6-ounce cans low-sodium chunk white tuna, drained
- 1 medium red or yellow sweet pepper, cut into thin strips
- 1 cup fresh snow pea pods, trimmed and halved crosswise
- ¼ cup sliced green onions
- 1 recipe Ginger Vinaigrette (right)
- 2 tablespoons chopped cashews

1. In a very large bowl, combine cabbage, tuna, sweet pepper, pea pods, and green onions. Gently toss to mix.

2. Pour Ginger Vinaigrette over cabbage mixture; toss to coat. Serve immediately or cover and chill up to 12 hours. Sprinkle with cashews before serving.

GINGER VINAIGRETTE: In a screw-top jar, combine ½ cup rice vinegar, 1 tablespoon sugar, 1 tablespoon reduced-sodium soy sauce, 1 teaspoon toasted sesame oil, ¼ teaspoon ground ginger, and ⅛ to ¼ teaspoon crushed red pepper. Cover and shake well.

PER SERVING: 268 cal., 9 g total fat (2 g sat. fat), 43 mg chol., 205 mg sodium, 14 g carb., 3 g fiber, 30 g pro. Exchanges: 2 vegetable, 4 lean meat, 1 fat. Carb choices: 1.

Pollock with Nectarine Salsa

The citrusy nectarine-and-kiwi salsa brings out the mild, natural sweetness of the pollock. If pollock isn't available, substitute cod.

SERVINGS 2 (1½ cups greens, 4 ounces fish, and ½ cup salsa each)

CARB. PER SERVING 15 g

Pollock with Nectarine Salsa

- 8 ounces fresh or frozen pollock fillet, cut about 1 inch thick
- 1 recipe Nectarine Salsa (below)
- ½ teaspoon olive oil
- ¼ teaspoon freshly ground black pepper
- 3 cups torn mixed salad greens

1. Thaw fish, if frozen. Prepare Nectarine Salsa.

2. Rinse fish; pat dry with paper towels. Rub oil over both sides of fish; sprinkle with pepper. Place fish in a well-greased grill basket. For a charcoal grill, place basket on the grill rack directly over medium coals. Grill, uncovered, for 8 to 12 minutes or until fish flakes easily when tested with a fork, turning once. (For a gas grill, preheat grill. Reduce heat to medium. Place fish on grill rack over heat. Cover and grill as above.)

3. To serve, divide greens between two shallow bowls. Break up fish into large pieces and place on top of greens. Top with Nectarine Salsa.

NECTARINE SALSA: In a small bowl, combine 1 small nectarine, cut into ½-inch pieces; ½ of a small cucumber, seeded and cut into ½-inch pieces; ½ of a kiwifruit, peeled and cut into ½-inch pieces; 2 tablespoons thinly sliced green onion; 2 tablespoons orange juice; and 1 teaspoon vinegar. Cover and chill until ready to serve.

PER SERVING: 181 cal., 3 g total fat (0 g sat. fat), 81 mg chol., 111 mg sodium, 15 g carb., 3 g fiber, 24 g pro. Exchanges: 2 vegetable, 0.5 fruit, 3 lean meat. Carb choices: 1.

Shrimp and Watermelon Salad

If you purchase a portion of watermelon instead of a whole melon, use the equivalent of a half slice for each serving.

SERVINGS 4 (1 cup shrimp-vegetable mixture and 1 piece watermelon each)

CARB. PER SERVING 16 g

- 2 tablespoons olive oil
- 1 pound peeled, deveined medium shrimp
- 2 teaspoons snipped fresh thyme
- 4 cups sliced bok choy or napa cabbage
- 1 cup grape tomatoes, halved
  Salt
  Black pepper
- 2 1-inch slices seedless watermelon, halved
  Small limes, halved
- ¼ cup crumbled reduced-fat feta cheese (optional)
  Fresh thyme sprigs

1. In a large skillet, heat 1 tablespoon of the oil over medium-high heat. Add shrimp; cook and stir about 3 minutes or until shrimp are opaque. Transfer shrimp to a bowl; stir in thyme. Add remaining olive oil, bok choy, and tomatoes to skillet; cook and stir for 1 minute. Return shrimp to skillet; cook and stir for 1 minute more. Season with salt and pepper.

2. Serve shrimp and vegetables with watermelon. Squeeze lime juice on salads. If desired, sprinkle with feta and garnish with thyme sprigs.

PER SERVING: 241 cal., 9 g total fat (1 g sat. fat), 172 mg chol., 363 mg sodium, 16 g carb., 2 g fiber, 25 g pro. Exchanges: 1 vegetable, 0.5 fruit, 3 lean meat, 1 fat. Carb choices: 1.

Shrimp and
Watermelon Salad

Lobster and Citrus Salad

Confetti Barley Salad

Lobster and Citrus Salad

Blood oranges, available December through July, give this salad a visual boost. Although their skin appears a bit darker than a regular orange, it's their ruby red flesh and rich orange flavor that makes them so spectacular.

SERVINGS 4

CARB. PER SERVING 20 g

4 8-ounce frozen lobster tails, thawed
3 blood oranges or regular oranges
   Blood orange juice or orange juice
8 cups mesclun greens or other salad greens
2 shallots, finely chopped
3 tablespoons canola oil
2 tablespoons grapefruit juice or orange juice
2 teaspoons snipped fresh thyme or ¼ teaspoon dried thyme, crushed
   Freshly ground black pepper (optional)

1. In a 3-quart saucepan, bring 6 cups *water* and 1 teaspoon *salt* to boiling. Add lobster. Simmer, uncovered, for 8 to 12 minutes or until shells turn bright red and meat is tender. Drain; let stand until cool enough to handle.

2. Meanwhile, peel and section oranges over a small bowl to catch juices. Add enough additional juice to make ⅓ cup; set aside. In a large bowl, toss together the salad greens and orange sections. Divide the salad mixture among four dinner plates

3. For dressing: In a medium skillet, cook shallots in hot oil until tender. Carefully add the ⅓ cup orange juice, the 2 tablespoons grapefruit juice, and the thyme. Bring to boiling; keep warm.

4. To remove lobster meat from shell, insert a fork and push the tail meat out in one piece. Remove and discard the black vein that runs the length of the tail meat. Slice the tail meat, making ½-inch medallions. Arrange lobster medallions on top of greens. Spoon dressing over salads. If desired, sprinkle with pepper. Serve immediately.

PER SERVING: 302 cal., 12 g total fat (1 g sat. fat), 135 mg chol., 436 mg sodium, 20 g carb., 4 g fiber, 29 g pro. Exchanges: 1.5 vegetable, 1 fruit, 3.5 lean meat, 1 fat. Carb choices: 1.

Confetti Barley Salad

Succotash is simply a combination of beans and corn. If you can't find frozen succatash, substitute 1 cup each whole kernel corn and lima beans.

SERVINGS 6

CARB. PER SERVING 38 g

5 cups water
1 cup pearl barley
2 cups frozen succotash, thawed
¼ cup white wine vinegar
3 tablespoons olive oil
1 tablespoon Dijon-style mustard
2 teaspoons snipped fresh oregano or ½ teaspoon dried oregano, crushed
2 cloves garlic, minced
½ teaspoon salt
¼ teaspoon black pepper
1 cup finely chopped red sweet pepper
⅓ cup sliced pitted ripe olives
   Fresh herb sprigs (optional)

1. In a large saucepan, bring the water to boiling. Stir in barley; reduce heat. Cover and simmer for 45 to 50 minutes or just until barley is tender, adding succotash for the last 10 minutes of cooking; drain. Rinse with cold water; drain again.

2. Meanwhile, for dressing: In a screw-top jar, combine vinegar, oil, mustard, oregano, garlic, salt, and black pepper. Cover and shake well. Set aside.

3. In a large bowl, stir together the barley mixture, sweet pepper, and olives. Shake dressing. Pour the dressing over barley mixture; toss gently to coat. Serve immediately or cover and refrigerate for up to 24 hours. If desired, garnish with fresh herb sprigs.

PER SERVING: 247 cal., 8 g total fat (1 g sat. fat), 0 mg chol., 363 mg sodium, 38 g carb., 5 g fiber, 6 g pro. Exchanges: 2.5 starch, 1 fat. Carb choices: 2.5.

▶ QUICK TIP

This bulgur, bean, and vegetable salad is loaded with fiber. Fiber has been shown to slow glucose absorption, and soluble fiber can help lower cholesterol.

Tabbouleh with Edamame and Feta

Tabbouleh with Edamame and Feta

This zesty Mediterranean salad makes a great vegetarian main dish. Or serve ½-cup portions as a side dish with broiled or grilled chicken, beef, or pork.

SERVINGS 6 (about 1¼ cups each)
CARB. PER SERVING 34 g

2½ cups water
1¼ cups bulgur
¼ cup lemon juice
3 tablespoons purchased basil pesto
2 cups fresh or thawed frozen shelled sweet soybeans (edamame)
2 cups cherry tomatoes, cut up
⅓ cup crumbled reduced-fat feta cheese
⅓ cup thinly sliced green onions
2 tablespoons snipped fresh parsley
¼ teaspoon black pepper
Fresh parsley sprigs (optional)

1. In a medium saucepan, bring the water to boiling; add uncooked bulgur. Return to boiling; reduce heat. Simmer, covered, for 15 minutes or until most of the liquid is absorbed. Remove from heat. Transfer to a bowl.
2. In a small bowl, whisk together lemon juice and pesto. Add to bulgur along with soybeans, cherry tomatoes, feta cheese, green onions, the snipped parsley, and pepper. Toss gently to combine. Serve immediately or cover and chill for up to 4 hours. If desired, garnish with parsley sprigs.

PER SERVING: 266 cal., 10 g total fat (1 g sat. fat), 3 mg chol., 181 mg sodium, 34 g carb., 9 g fiber, 14 g pro. Exchanges: 0.5 vegetable, 2 starch, 1 medium-fat meat, 0.5 fat. Carb choices: 2.

Layered Southwestern Salad with Tortilla Strips

Break out of a salad rut with this zesty, slimmed-down Tex-Mex medley topped off with a light sour cream dressing and homemade tortilla chips.

SERVINGS 6 (about 2 cups each)
CARB. PER SERVING 29 g

2 6-inch corn tortillas
Nonstick cooking spray
½ cup light sour cream
¼ cup snipped fresh cilantro
2 tablespoons fat-free milk
1 teaspoon olive oil
1 large clove garlic, minced
½ teaspoon chili powder
½ teaspoon finely shredded lime peel
¼ teaspoon salt
¼ teaspoon black pepper
6 cups torn romaine
4 roma tomatoes, chopped (2 cups)
1 15-ounce can black beans, rinsed and drained
1 cup fresh corn kernels*
½ cup shredded reduced-fat cheddar cheese (2 ounces)
1 avocado, halved, pitted, peeled, and chopped
Snipped fresh cilantro (optional)

1. Preheat oven to 350°F. Cut tortillas into ½-inch-wide strips; place in a 15×10×1-inch baking pan. Coat tortillas lightly with cooking spray. Bake for 15 to 18 minutes or just until crisp, stirring once. Cool on a wire rack.
2. For dressing: In a small bowl, stir together sour cream, the ¼ cup cilantro, the milk, oil, garlic, chili power, lime peel, salt, and pepper.
3. Place lettuce in a large glass serving bowl. Top with tomatoes, beans, corn, cheese, and avocado. Add dressing and sprinkle with tortilla strips. If desired, garnish with additional cilantro.

*TEST KITCHEN TIP: It isn't necessary to cook the corn. However, for a roasted flavor and softer texture, try baking it with the tortilla strips. Place the strips at one end of the baking pan and the corn at the other end.

PER SERVING: 227 cal., 11 g total fat (3 g sat. fat), 12 mg chol., 386 mg sodium, 29 g carb., 9 g fiber, 11 g pro. Exchanges: 1.5 vegetable, 1 starch, 0.5 lean meat, 2 fat. Carb choices: 2.

Layered Southwestern
Salad with Tortilla Strips

comforting
soups and stews

Cozying up to a bowl of hearty soup provides delicious comfort. To make this classic comfort food diabetes-friendly, we cut salt, fat, and calories and pumped up the taste with flavorful ingredients. Whether you like a brothy soup, a chunky stew, or a spunky chili, you'll find a favorite here.

Indian Vegetable Soup

When selecting an eggplant, look for one that is plump, glossy, and heavy. Skip any with scarred, bruised, or dull surfaces.

SERVINGS 6 (1½ cups each)
CARB. PER SERVING 38 g

- 1 medium eggplant, cut into ½-inch cubes (5 to 6 cups)
- 1 14-ounce can vegetable broth
- 1 pound tiny new potatoes, cut into 1-inch pieces
- 2 cups chopped tomatoes or one 14.5-ounce can no-salt-added diced tomatoes, undrained
- 1¾ cups water
- 1 15-ounce can garbanzo beans (chickpeas), rinsed and drained
- 2 teaspoons grated fresh ginger or ½ teaspoon ground ginger
- 1½ teaspoons curry powder
- 1 teaspoon ground coriander
- ¼ teaspoon salt
- ¼ teaspoon black pepper
  Fresh cilantro sprigs

1. In a 5- to 6-quart slow cooker, combine eggplant, broth, potatoes, tomatoes, the water, garbanzo beans, ginger, curry powder, coriander, salt, and pepper.
2. Cover and cook on low-heat setting for 9 to 10 hours or on high-heat setting for 4½ to 5 hours.
3. To serve, ladle soup into bowls. Garnish each serving with a cilantro sprig.
PER SERVING: 182 cal., 1 g total fat (0 g sat. fat), 0 mg chol., 578 mg sodium, 38 g carb., 9 g fiber, 7 g pro. Exchanges: 1 vegetable, 2 starch. Carb choices: 2.5.

Carrot-Cucmber
Gazpacho

2. To serve, ladle soup into bowls or glasses. Add the cut-up radishes. If desired, top with additional shredded arugula, radishes, and corn, and pass lime wedges.

*TEST KITCHEN TIP: Color of gazpacho may vary with the ripeness and variety of the tomatoes used.

PER SERVING: 66 cal., 0 g total fat, 0 mg chol., 270 mg sodium, 15 g carb., 2 g fiber, 2 g pro. Exchanges: 1.5 vegetable, 0.5 carb. Carb choices: 1.

Curried Corn Soup

This creamy soup gives you a triple dose of soy because it's made with soybean oil, soymilk, and soy yogurt.

SERVINGS 8 (¾ cup each)
CARB. PER SERVING 21 g

½   cup finely chopped green sweet pepper
½   cup finely chopped red sweet pepper
¼   cup finely chopped onion
2   teaspoons canola oil
2   teaspoons curry powder
¼   teaspoon salt
3   cups fresh corn kernels (6 ears) or one 16-ounce
      package frozen whole kernel corn, thawed
1   cup reduced-sodium chicken broth
¼   teaspoon black pepper
3   cups plain light soymilk
2   tablespoons snipped fresh cilantro
⅓   cup plain soy yogurt or plain low-fat yogurt
      Fresh cilantro leaves

1. In a large saucepan, cook sweet peppers and onion in hot oil over medium-high heat about 4 minutes or until tender, stirring occasionally. Add curry powder and salt; cook and stir for 1 minute more.

2. Stir in corn, broth, and black pepper. Bring to boiling; reduce heat. Simmer, covered, about 5 minutes or until corn is tender.

3. Transfer 2 cups of the corn mixture to a blender or food processor. Add ½ cup of the soymilk. Cover and blend or process until mixture is nearly smooth. Return pureed mixture to saucepan; stir in the remaining 2½ cups soymilk. Cook over medium heat, stirring gently, until heated through. Stir in the snipped cilantro.

4. To serve, ladle soup into bowls. Top each serving with yogurt and cilantro leaves.

PER SERVING: 118 cal., 3 g total fat (0 g sat. fat), 0 mg chol., 181 mg sodium, 21 g carb., 2 g fiber, 5 g pro. Exchanges: 0.5 milk, 0.5 starch, 0.5 carb. Carb choices: 1.5.

Carrot-Cucumber Gazpacho

If you like horseradish, use 2 tablespoons in this chilled soup.

SERVINGS 5 (1 cup each)
CARB. PER SERVING 15 g

2   large tomatoes (about 1 pound), quartered and seeded*
1½   cups carrot juice
2   tablespoons coarsely chopped fresh chives
1   medium cucumber, seeded and coarsely chopped
      (1½ cups)
1½   cups fresh corn kernels (3 ears) (optional)
¼   of a jicama, peeled and chopped (1 cup)
½   cup shredded arugula
1   to 2 tablespoons prepared horseradish
4   large or 6 small radishes, quartered or cut into chunks
      Shredded arugula (optional)
      Coarsely chopped radishes (optional)
      Fresh corn (optional)
      Lime wedges (optional)

1. For soup: In a blender or food processor, combine tomatoes, carrot juice, and chives. Cover and blend or process until smooth. Transfer mixture to a large bowl. Stir in cucumber, the 1½ cups corn (if desired), the jicama, the ½ cup arugula, the horseradish, and ½ teaspoon *salt*. Cover and chill at least 1 hour or up to 24 hours before serving.

Quinoa (pronounced KEEN-wa) requires rinsing to remove residue. Because it is a fine-texture grain, place it in a fine-mesh sieve to rinse under cool running water.

Squash and Quinoa Soup

The apricot nectar and butternut squash turn this hearty vegetable blend into a pot of gold.

SERVINGS 6 (1⅓ cups each)

CARB. PER SERVING 30 g

- 12 ounces skinless, boneless chicken breast halves, cut into 1-inch pieces
- ⅓ cup finely chopped shallots or onion
- 2 teaspoons olive oil or canola oil
- 2 14-ounce cans reduced-sodium chicken broth
- 1 5.5-ounce can apricot nectar
- 1 pound butternut squash, peeled, halved, seeded, and cut into 1-inch cubes
- ¾ cup quinoa, rinsed and drained
- 1 teaspoon ground cumin
- 2 small zucchini, halved lengthwise and cut into 1-inch pieces
- ⅛ teaspoon salt
- ⅛ teaspoon black pepper

1. In a large saucepan, cook chicken and shallots in hot oil over medium heat for 2 to 3 minutes or until shallots are tender, stirring occasionally. Carefully add broth, apricot nectar, squash, uncooked quinoa, and cumin. Bring to boiling; reduce heat. Simmer, covered, for 5 minutes. Add zucchini. Cover and cook about 10 minutes more or until squash and quinoa are tender. Stir in salt and pepper.

2. To serve, ladle soup into bowls.

PER SERVING: 224 cal., 4 g total fat (1 g sat. fat), 33 mg chol., 403 mg sodium, 30 g carb., 4 g fiber, 19 g pro. Exchanges: 0.5 vegetable, 1.5 starch, 2 lean meat. Carb choices: 2.

Squash and Quinoa Soup

Mustard-Herb Beef Stew

To cut carbs, serve this hearty bowl without the crusty bread slices.

SERVINGS 8 (about 1¼ cups each)
CARB. PER SERVING 36 g

- ⅓ cup all-purpose flour
- 1 tablespoon snipped fresh Italian (flat-leaf) parsley
- 1 teaspoon snipped fresh thyme or ½ teaspoon dried thyme, crushed
- 1 teaspoon black pepper
- ¼ teaspoon salt
- 1½ pounds boneless beef chuck, cut into 1-inch pieces
- 2 tablespoons olive oil
- 1 8- to 10-ounce package cipolini onions, peeled, or 1 medium onion, peeled and cut into wedges
- 4 carrots, peeled and cut into 1-inch pieces
- 1 8-ounce package cremini mushrooms, halved if large
- 8 small new Yukon gold potatoes, halved
- 3 tablespoons tomato paste
- 2 tablespoons spicy brown mustard
- 1 14-ounce can lower-sodium beef broth
- 1 12-ounce bottle dark porter beer or nonalocholic beer
- 1 bay leaf
- Crusty bread slices

1. In large bowl or plastic bag, combine flour, parsley, thyme, pepper, and salt. Add beef, a few pieces at a time; stir or shake to coat. Reserve leftover flour mixture.

2. In a 6-quart Dutch oven, brown beef in hot oil over medium-high heat. Stir in onions, carrots, mushrooms, and potatoes. Cook and stir for 3 minutes. Stir in tomato paste, mustard, and the remaining flour mixture. Add broth, beer, and bay leaf. Bring to boiling; reduce heat. Simmer, covered, for 1 to 1¼ hours or until beef is tender. Discard bay leaf. Serve with crusty bread.

PER SERVING: 338 cal., 8 g total fat (2 g sat. fat), 37 mg chol., 538 mg sodium, 36 g carb., 4 g fiber, 25 g pro. Exchanges: 1 vegetable, 2 starch, 2.5 lean meat, 1 fat. Carb choices: 2.5.

Skillet
Beef Stew

Skillet Beef Stew

This is old-fashioned goodness—chunky beef and vegetables smothered in a rich, gravylike mixture and served over mashed potatoes.

SERVINGS 8 (about ½ cup potatoes and 1 cup stew each)
CARB. PER SERVING 40 g

- 2 tablespoons canola oil
- 2 pounds beef stew meat, cut into 1-inch cubes
- 2 teaspoons dried thyme or oregano, crushed
- ¼ teaspoon black pepper
- 6 medium carrots, peeled and cut into quarters (1 pound)
- 4 stalks celery, trimmed and cut into 2-inch pieces
- 2 medium onions, peeled and cut into ½-inch slices
- 6 cups lower-sodium beef broth
- ⅓ cup all-purpose flour
- 8 medium Yukon gold potatoes, scrubbed (about 2¾ pounds)
- 1 cup fat-free milk or buttermilk
- ½ teaspoon black pepper
- ¼ teaspoon salt
  Cracked black pepper

1. In a very skillet, heat oil over medium-high heat; add beef. Sprinkle with thyme and the ¼ teaspoon pepper. Cook and stir until browned on all sides. Remove from skillet using a slotted spoon; set aside. Add carrots, celery, and onions to skillet. Cook and stir over medium heat for 5 minutes. Return beef to pan. In a large bowl, whisk together broth and flour. Stir broth mixture into pan. Bring to boiling; reduce heat. Simmer, covered, for 45 minutes. Uncover and simmer for 10 to 15 minutes more or until beef and vegetables are tender.
2. Meanwhile, place four of the potatoes in a large microwave-safe bowl. Cover with vented lid or plastic wrap. Cook potatoes on high (100% power) for 8 minutes. Carefully remove bowl from microwave oven. Set cooked potatoes aside. Repeat with remaining potatoes. Return all potatoes to the large bowl. Break up any larger potatoes with the back of a wooden spoon. Add milk, pepper, and the ¼ teaspoon salt. Using a potato masher, mash until nearly smooth.
3. To serve, spread potatoes to cover bottom of each serving bowl. Spoon stew on top of potatoes. Sprinkle each serving with cracked black pepper.

PER SERVING: 375 cal., 10 g total fat (2 g sat. fat), 62 mg chol., 557 mg sodium, 40 g carb., 6 g fiber, 32 g pro. Exchanges: 1 vegetable, 2 starch, 3.5 lean meat, 0.5 fat. Carb choices: 2.5.

Bowl O' Red Chili

Texans have strong opinions about their chili. The meat must be cubed, never ground. Beans may be served alongside but are never stirred into the mixture; neither are canned tomatoes.

SERVINGS 8 (about 1 cup each)
CARB. PER SERVING 14 g

- 3 pounds boneless lean beef chuck, cut into ½-inch cubes
- 1 tablespoon canola oil
- 4 large onions, chopped (3 cups)
- 3 tablespoons chili powder
- 3 tablespoons yellow cornmeal
- 6 cloves garlic, minced
- 1 tablespoon ground cumin
- 2 teaspoons dried oregano, crushed
- ¼ teaspoon cayenne pepper
- 1 14-ounce can lower-sodium beef broth
- 1 tablespoon packed brown sugar

1. Sprinkle beef with ½ teaspoon *salt* and ¼ teaspoon *black pepper*. In a Dutch oven, brown beef, one-third at a time, in hot oil. (Add more oil during cooking, if necessary.) Remove beef from Dutch oven.
2. Add onions to Dutch oven; cook over medium-high heat about 5 minutes or until tender. Stir in chili powder, cornmeal, garlic, cumin, oregano, and cayenne pepper; cook for 30 seconds.
3. Stir in browned beef, broth, 1¼ cups *water*, brown sugar, ¼ teaspoon *salt*, and ¼ teaspoon *black pepper*. Bring to boiling; reduce heat. Simmer, covered, for 1½ to 2 hours or until meat is tender. If desired, top each serving with additional chopped onion.

PER SERVING: 333 cal., 12 g total fat (3 g sat. fat), 80 mg chol., 376 mg sodium, 14 g carb., 3 g fiber, 40 g pro. Exchanges: 0.5 vegetable, 0.5 starch, 5 lean meat, 1 fat. Carb choices: 1.

Southwestern Noodle Bowl

If you prefer foods on the mild side, choose a mild to medium salsa instead of the hot-style salsa.

SERVINGS 8 (1 cup each)
CARB. PER SERVING 21 g

1½ pounds beef flank steak or beef top round steak, cut into thin bite-size strips
1 teaspoon ground cumin
¼ teaspoon salt
⅛ teaspoon black pepper
2 tablespoons canola oil
2 cloves garlic, minced
2 14-ounce cans lower-sodium beef broth
1 14-ounce can reduced-sodium chicken broth
6 ounces dried angel hair pasta
2 medium red or yellow sweet peppers, chopped
6 green onions, trimmed and bias-sliced into 1-inch pieces
½ cup purchased hot-style salsa
¼ cup snipped fresh oregano
Purchased salsa (optional)
California pepper mix or pepper seasoning (optional)

1. Season meat with cumin, salt, and pepper; set aside.
2. Pour 1 tablespoon of the oil into a wok or very large skillet. Preheat over medium-high heat. Add garlic; stir-fry for 15 seconds. Add half of the beef and stir-fry for 2 to 3 minutes or until no longer pink. Remove and repeat with remaining oil and beef. Return all of the beef to the wok or skillet. Add broth; bring to boiling.
3. Add pasta, sweet peppers, and green onions to mixture in wok; return to boiling. Cook, uncovered, for 3 minutes or until pasta is tender, stirring occasionally. Stir in the ½ cup salsa and the oregano; heat through.
4. To serve, ladle mixture into shallow soup bowls. If desired, swirl pasta into nests in bowls; top with additional salsa, and sprinkle with pepper mix.
PER SERVING: 260 cal., 9 g total fat (2 g sat. fat), 28 mg chol., 616 mg sodium, 21 g carb., 2 g fiber, 24 g pro. Exchanges: 0.5 vegetable, 1 starch, 3 lean meat, 0.5 fat. Carb choices: 1.5.

Mexican-Style Chicken Soup

Although red sweet pepper matches the ruby hue of the broth, any color of sweet pepper will do.

SERVINGS 6 (1⅔ cups each)
CARB. PER SERVING 19 g

1 large red sweet pepper, seeded and chopped (1 cup)
1 large onion, chopped (¾ cup)
2 teaspoons canola oil
1½ teaspoons chili powder
1 teaspoon ground cumin
2 14-ounce cans reduced-sodium chicken broth
1¾ cups water
1½ cups peeled and seeded winter squash cut into ½-inch pieces
1 14.5-ounce can Mexican-style stewed tomatoes, undrained, cut up
2 cups chopped cooked chicken or turkey (10 ounces)
1 cup frozen whole kernel corn
¼ cup snipped fresh cilantro (optional)

1. In a 4-quart Dutch oven, cook sweet pepper and onion in hot oil over medium heat about 5 minutes or until tender, stirring occasionally. Stir in chili powder and cumin; cook and stir for 30 seconds.
2. Carefully add broth, the water, squash, and undrained tomatoes. Bring to boiling; reduce heat. Simmer, covered, about 20 minutes or until squash is tender, stirring occasionally. Stir in chicken and corn. Heat through. If desired, sprinkle with cilantro.
PER SERVING: 180 cal., 4 g total fat (1 g sat. fat), 40 mg chol., 594 mg sodium, 19 g carb., 2 g fiber, 19 g pro. Exchanges: 1 vegetable, 1 starch, 2 lean meat. Carb choices: 1.

Southwestern Noodle Bowl

QUICK TIP

To easily chop canned tomatoes, leave the tomatoes in the can and use short, quick strokes with kitchen scissors to cut desired-size pieces.

Mexican-Style
Chicken Soup

Sage Chicken Dumpling Soup

Use a flatware tablespoon to scoop up the dumpling dough, then push it onto the soup with a rubber spatula.

SERVINGS 8 (about 1¼ cups each)

CARB. PER SERVING 37 g

- 2 cups sliced fresh mushrooms
- 1 cup chopped onions (2 medium)
- 1 tablespoon olive oil
- ¼ cup all-purpose flour
- 4 cups reduced-sodium chicken broth
- 4 cups coarsely chopped cooked chicken
- 2 cups frozen peas
- ¼ cup pitted kalamata olives, halved
- 1 tablespoon lemon juice
- 1 teaspoon ground sage
- 1 recipe Buttermilk Dumplings (right)
  Thinly sliced green onion (optional)
  Fried Sage Sprigs (right) (optional)

1. In a 4-quart Dutch oven, cook mushrooms and onions in hot oil over medium heat for 6 to 8 minutes or until mushrooms are tender and liquid has evaporated.

2. Stir in flour until combined. Add broth and 2 cups water all at once. Cook and stir until thickened and bubbly. Stir in chicken, peas, olives, lemon juice, and sage. Return to boiling. Drop Buttermilk Dumplings batter in eight mounds on top of bubbly soup. Simmer, covered, for 10 minutes or until a toothpick inserted near a dumpling center comes out clean. Remove pan from heat. If desired, sprinkle individual servings with green onions and top with Fried Sage Sprigs.

BUTTERMILK DUMPLINGS: In a bowl, combine 2 cups all-purpose flour, ½ teaspoon baking powder, ¼ teaspoon baking soda, and ¼ teaspoon salt. Stir in ¼ cup sliced green onions and 1 tablespoon snipped fresh Italian (flat-leaf) parsley. Add 1 cup buttermilk and 2 tablespoons olive oil or cooking oil and stir until just moistened.

PER SERVING: 375 cal., 12 g total fat (2 g sat. fat), 64 mg chol., 633 mg sodium, 37 g carb., 3 g fiber, 30 g pro. Exchanges: 0.5 vegetable, 2 starch, 3.5 lean meat, 1 fat. Carb choices: 2.5.

FRIED SAGE SPRIGS: In a medium saucepan, heat ¼ cup olive oil over medium heat until hot but not smoky. Add 8 small sage sprigs, 2 at a time, and cook for 30 to 60 seconds or until crisp. Remove with a slotted spoon and drain on paper towels.

Choose-a-Vegetable
Chicken and Pasta Soup

Choose-a-Vegetable Chicken and Pasta Soup

Here's an excuse to clean out the vegetable drawer of your refrigerator. Chop a mix of veggies into equal-size pieces for a different soup every time you make it.

SERVINGS 6 (1¼ cups each)

CARB. PER SERVING 16 g

- 2 14-ounce cans reduced-sodium chicken broth
- 2 cups water
- 1 tablespoon snipped fresh basil or 1 teaspoon dried basil, crushed
- ¼ teaspoon black pepper
- 1 cup dried multigrain or regular elbow macaroni
- 3 cups vegetables, such as thinly sliced carrots, packaged broccoli florets, and/or chopped green or red sweet peppers
- 1½ cups cubed cooked chicken breast (about 8 ounces)
- ¼ cup finely shredded Parmesan cheese (1 ounce)

1. In a Dutch oven, combine broth, water, dried basil (if using), and black pepper; bring to boiling. Stir in pasta. Return to boiling; reduce heat. Simmer, covered, for 5 minutes. Stir in vegetables. Return to boiling; reduce heat. Simmer, covered, for 5 to 8 minutes more or until vegetables and pasta are tender. Stir in chicken; heat through. Stir in fresh basil (if using).

2. To serve, ladle soup into bowls. Top individual servings with Parmesan cheese.

PER SERVING: 161 cal., 3 g total fat (1 g sat. fat), 34 mg chol., 420 mg sodium, 16 g carb., 3 g fiber, 18 g pro. Exchanges: 0.5 vegetable, 1 starch, 2 lean meat. Carb choices: 1.

Chipotle-Chicken Chowder

Chipotles (dried smoked jalapeño peppers) add both heat and a distinctive sweet, almost cocoalike flavor to this creamy south-of-the-border chowder. You'll find canned chipotle peppers in adobo sauce in the supermarket or at a Mexican foods market.

SERVINGS 4 (about 1¾ cups each)

CARB. PER SERVING 35 g

- 2 red and/or green sweet peppers, chopped (1½ cups)
- 1 large onion, chopped (¾ cup)
- ¼ teaspoon ground cumin
- 1 tablespoon olive oil
- 1 14-ounce can reduced-sodium chicken broth
- 2 cups cubed, peeled potatoes
- ½ cup water
- 1 to 2 teaspoons chopped canned chipotle peppers in adobo sauce
- 1½ cups chopped cooked chicken (about 8 ounces)
- 1 12-ounce can evaporated fat-free milk
- 3 tablespoons cornstarch
  Sliced green onions (optional)

1. In a large saucepan, cook sweet peppers, chopped onion, and cumin in hot oil over medium-high heat for 3 minutes, stirring occasionally.

2. Carefully add chicken broth, potatoes, the water, and chipotle peppers. Bring to boiling; reduce heat. Simmer, covered, about 8 minutes or until potatoes are tender. Stir in chicken.

3. Gradually stir about ⅓ cup of the milk into cornstarch in a small bowl; stir into broth mixture in saucepan. Add the remaining milk. Cook and stir over medium heat until thickened and bubbly. Cook and stir for 2 minutes more. If desired, garnish individual servings with sliced green onions.

PER SERVING: 313 cal., 8 g total fat (2 g sat. fat), 50 mg chol., 394 mg sodium, 35 g carb., 3 g fiber, 25 g pro. Exchanges: 0.5 vegetable, 2 starch, 2.5 lean meat, 0.5 fat. Carb choices: 2.

French Chicken Stew

If there's room in your meal plan, mop up this tomatoey stew with a slice of French bread.

SERVINGS 8 (about 1⅓ cups each)
CARB. PER SERVING 17 g

- 4 cups sliced button and/or shiitake mushrooms
- 1 14.5-ounce can diced tomatoes, undrained
- 2 medium carrots, thinly bias-sliced (1 cup)
- 1 medium onion, chopped (½ cup)
- 1 medium round red potato, cut into 1-inch pieces
- ½ cup 1-inch pieces fresh green beans
- ⅓ cup pitted ripe olives, halved
- 1 cup reduced-sodium chicken broth
- ½ cup dry white wine or reduced-sodium chicken broth
- 2 tablespoons quick-cooking tapioca
- 1 teaspoon herbes de Provence or dried Italian seasoning, crushed
- ¾ teaspoon dried thyme, crushed
- ¼ teaspoon coarsely ground black pepper
- 8 skinless, boneless chicken thighs (1¾ to 2 pounds total)
- ½ teaspoon seasoned salt
- 1 14-ounce jar tomato pasta sauce or one 16-ounce jar Alfredo pasta sauce

1. In a 5- to 6-quart slow cooker, combine mushrooms, tomatoes, carrots, onion, potato, green beans, olives, broth, wine, tapioca, herbes de Provence, thyme, and pepper. Place chicken on top; sprinkle with seasoned salt. Cover and cook on low-heat setting for 6 to 7 hours or on high-heat setting for 3 to 4 hours. Stir in pasta sauce.

2. To serve, ladle stew into bowls.

PER SERVING: 213 cal., 5 g total fat (1 g sat. fat), 82 mg chol., 556 mg sodium, 17 g carb., 4 g fiber, 23 g pro. Exchanges: 1.5 vegetable, 0.5 starch, 2.5 lean meat, 0.5 fat. Carb choices: 1.

French Chicken Stew

Chicken Stew with Tortellini

Dress up leftover chicken by stirring it into this quick-prep stew. Chunks of yellow squash and sweet pepper accompany plump tortellini and spinach.

SERVINGS 6 (1⅓ cups each)
CARB. PER SERVING 17 g

- 1½ cups water
- 2 14-ounce cans reduced-sodium chicken broth
- 1 medium yellow summer squash, halved lengthwise and cut into ½-inch slices
- 1 green sweet pepper, coarsely chopped (¾ cup)
- 1 cup dried cheese-filled tortellini pasta
- 2 medium carrots, sliced (1 cup)
- 1 medium onion, cut into thin wedges
- ¼ teaspoon garlic-pepper seasoning
- 2½ cups chopped cooked chicken breast
- 2 cups torn fresh spinach
- 2 tablespoons snipped fresh basil

1. In a Dutch oven, bring water and chicken broth to boiling. Add squash, sweet pepper, pasta, carrots, onion, and garlic-pepper seasoning. Return to boiling; reduce heat. Simmer, covered, about 15 minutes or until pasta and vegetables are nearly tender.

2. Stir in chicken. Cook, covered, about 5 minutes more or until pasta and vegetables are tender. Stir spinach and basil into stew.

3. To serve, ladle stew into bowls.

PER SERVING: 206 cal., 4 g total fat (1 g sat. fat), 50 mg chol., 561 mg sodium, 17 g carb., 2 g fiber, 25 g pro. Exchanges: 1 vegetable, 1 starch, 2.5 lean meat. Carb choices: 1.

Chicken Stew
with Tortellini

Turkey and Bean Chili

3. In a medium bowl, whisk together milk and flour until combined; stir into chicken mixture. Cook and stir until bubbly; cook and stir for 1 minute more. Sprinkle with parsley just before serving.

PER SERVING: 215 cal., 4 g total fat (1 g sat. fat), 53 mg chol., 560 mg sodium, 20 g carb., 2 g fiber, 25 g pro. Exchanges: 0.5 vegetable, 1 starch, 3 lean meat. Carb choices: 1.

Turkey and Bean Chili

If you want to spice up this mild chili, add a can of green chile peppers or a few smoked poblanos for more heat and smoky flavor.

SERVINGS 8 (about 1²/₃ cups each)
CARB. PER SERVING 34 g

- 2 stalks celery, thinly sliced (1 cup)
- 2 medium carrots, thinly sliced (1 cup)
- 1 medium onion, finely chopped (½ cup)
- 3 cloves garlic, minced
- 2 tablespoons chili powder
- 1 tablespoon olive oil
- 2 teaspoons ground cumin
- ½ teaspoon salt
- ½ teaspoon black pepper
- 2 15-ounce cans dark red kidney beans, rinsed and drained
- 1 pound ground turkey breast
- 5 14.5-ounce cans no-salt-added diced tomatoes, undrained
- 1 4-ounce can diced green chile peppers (optional)
- ½ cup shredded reduced-fat cheddar cheese (optional)

1. In an airtight storage container or resealable plastic bag, combine celery, carrots, onion, garlic, chili powder, oil, cumin, salt, and black pepper. Seal and chill for up to 24 hours. Place beans in a separate airtight storage container or resealable plastic bag. Seal and chill for up to 24 hours.

2. In a 6- to 8-quart Dutch oven, combine vegetable mixture and turkey. Cook until turkey is no longer pink and vegetables are tender, stirring occasionally to break up turkey. Stir in beans, undrained tomatoes, and, if desired, chile peppers. Bring to boiling; reduce heat. Simmer, covered, for 20 minutes, stirring occasionally.

3. If desired, sprinkle individual servings with cheese.

PER SERVING: 232 cal., 3 g total fat (1 g sat. fat), 23 mg chol., 502 mg sodium, 34 g carb., 12 g fiber, 23 g pro. Exchanges: 3.5 vegetable, 1 starch, 2 lean meat. Carb choices: 2.

Chicken-Squash Noodle Soup

Ceramic mugs make great serving bowls for this colorful take on all-time-favorite chicken noodle soup.

SERVINGS 6 (about 1½ cups each)
CARB. PER SERVING 20 g

- 1 pound skinless, boneless chicken breast halves, cut into 1-inch pieces
- ½ teaspoon poultry seasoning
- 1 tablespoon canola oil
- 1 medium onion, chopped (½ cup)
- 1 stalk celery chopped (½ cup)
- 1 medium carrot, peeled and chopped (½ cup)
- 2 cloves garlic, minced
- 3 14-ounce cans reduced-sodium chicken broth
- 1½ cups dried medium noodles
- 1 medium zucchini or yellow summer squash, quartered lengthwise and cut into 1-inch-thick pieces
- 1¾ cups fat-free milk
- ¼ cup all-purpose flour
- ¼ cup snipped fresh parsley

1. In a large bowl, combine chicken pieces and poultry seasoning; toss to coat. In a 4-quart Dutch oven, heat oil over medium heat. Add chicken pieces; cook for 3 to 5 minutes or until chicken pieces are browned. Using a slotted spoon, transfer chicken to bowl; set aside.

2. In the same Dutch oven, cook onion, celery, carrot, and garlic over medium heat about 5 minutes or just until tender, stirring occasionally. Add chicken broth; bring to boiling. Add chicken, noodles, and zucchini. Return to boiling; reduce heat. Cover and simmer for 5 minutes.

Spicy Pork and Vegetable Soup

This sophisticated and tasty soup is packed full of winter vegetables. Fresh spinach added prior to serving provides a touch of color and a nutrition boost.

SERVINGS 6 (about 1⅓ cups each)

CARB. PER SERVING 19 g

- 1 pound lean pork or beef stew meat, cut into ½-inch pieces
- 1 tablespoon canola oil
- 1 medium onion, chopped (½ cup)
- 1 teaspoon paprika
- 2 cloves garlic, minced
- 3 cups lower-sodium beef broth
- 8 ounces winter squash, peeled and cut into ½-inch pieces
- 3 medium parsnips or carrots, cut into ¼-inch slices (1½ cups)
- 1 medium sweet potato, peeled and cut into ½-inch pieces
- 1 8.75-ounce can whole kernel corn, undrained
- ¼ teaspoon salt
- ¼ teaspoon cayenne pepper
- 2 cups torn fresh spinach

1. In a large skillet, cook half of the meat in hot oil over medium heat until browned. Transfer meat to a 3½- or 4-quart slow cooker. Add the remaining meat, the onion, paprika, and garlic to skillet. Cook until meat is browned and onion is tender. Drain off fat. Transfer meat mixture to cooker.

2. Stir broth, squash, parsnips, sweet potato, corn, salt, and cayenne pepper into meat mixture in cooker. Cover and cook on low-heat setting for 10 to 11 hours or on high-heat setting for 5 to 5½ hours. Just before serving, stir in spinach.

3. To serve, ladle soup into bowls.

PER SERVING: 227 cal., 8 g total fat (2 g sat. fat), 41 mg chol., 488 mg sodium, 19 g carb., 4 g fiber, 20 g pro. Exchanges: 0.5 vegetable, 1 starch, 2.5 lean meat, 0.5 fat. Carb choices: 1.

Lamb and Orzo Soup

Curried-Cider Pork Stew

Top It

An edible garnish can turn a simple serving of soup into a stunning bowl. Try one of these tasty ideas.

1. **Swirl in a spoonful** of light sour cream.
2. **Sprinkle** with snipped fresh herbs.
3. **Add a few shreds** of fresh citrus peel.
4. **Crush up a couple** of reduced-fat crackers.
5. **Shake a light dusting of** spice over the top.
6. **Shred a little reduced-fat cheese** over each serving.
7. **Arrange a few slices** of seeded fresh jalapeño chile pepper on top of the soup.
8. **Sprinkle with thinly sliced** green onions or leeks.
9. **Using a vegetable peeler,** make some vegetable ribbons and add as a garnish.

Curried-Cider Pork Stew

*A popular food combo—pork and apples—
teams with curry powder, carrots, and butternut
squash for a different and delicious stew.*

SERVINGS 8 (about 1¼ cups each)
CARB. PER SERVING 27 g

2 pounds boneless pork shoulder
4 medium red and/or green crisp-tart cooking apples
1 tablespoon canola oil
1 large onion, cut into thin wedges
2 teaspoons curry powder
1 14-ounce can reduced-sodium chicken broth
⅔ cup apple cider or apple juice
¼ teaspoon salt
¼ teaspoon black pepper
12 ounces baby carrots with tops, trimmed, or packaged peeled baby carrots (2 cups)
2 stalks celery, sliced (1 cup)
1 1½-pound butternut squash, peeled, seeded, and cubed (2 cups)
Light sour cream, shredded orange peel, snipped fresh oregano, and/or freshly ground black pepper (optional)

1. Trim fat from pork; cut into 1-inch cubes. Peel, core, and chop two of the apples; set aside. In a 4-quart Dutch oven, brown pork, half at a time, in hot oil. Return all pork to pan; add chopped apples, onion, and curry powder. Cook and stir for 2 minutes. Add broth, cider, salt, and pepper. Bring to boiling; reduce heat and simmer, covered, for 30 minutes, stirring occasionally.
2. Add carrots and celery to pork mixture. Return to boiling; reduce heat. Simmer, covered, for 20 minutes, stirring occasionally. Meanwhile, cut remaining apples into ¼-inch-thick wedges; add to pan along with squash. Cover and cook for 10 to 12 minutes more or until pork and vegetables are tender.
3. To serve, ladle stew into bowls. If desired, top individual servings with sour cream, orange peel, oregano, and/or freshly ground pepper.
PER SERVING: 295 cal., 10 g total fat (3 g sat. fat), 76 mg chol., 311 mg sodium, 27 g carb., 5 g fiber, 24 g pro. Exchanges: 0.5 vegetable, 1 fruit, 0.5 starch, 3 lean meat, 1 fat. Carb choices: 2.

Lamb and Orzo Soup

*Braising lamb shanks, relatively tough cuts of meat,
transforms them into fork-tender morsels that
add flavor and richness to this soup.*

SERVINGS 6 (about 1½ cups each)
CARB. PER SERVING 20 g

2½ pounds lamb shanks
4 cups water
4 cups reduced-sodium chicken broth
2 bay leaves
1 tablespoon snipped fresh oregano or 1 teaspoon dried oregano, crushed
1½ teaspoons snipped fresh marjoram or ½ teaspoon dried marjoram, crushed
¼ teaspoon black pepper
2 medium carrots, peeled into thin ribbons or cut into short thin strips (1 cup)
2 stalks celery, sliced (1 cup)
¾ cup dried orzo
3 cups torn fresh spinach or ½ of a 10-ounce package frozen chopped spinach, thawed and well drained
Finely shredded Parmesan cheese (optional)

1. In a large Dutch oven, combine lamb shanks, the water, broth, bay leaves, oregano, marjoram, and pepper. Bring to boiling; reduce heat. Simmer, covered, for 1¼ to 1½ hours or until meat is tender.
2. Remove shanks from Dutch oven. When shanks are cool enough to handle, cut meat off bones; coarsely chop meat. Discard bones. Strain broth through a large sieve or colander lined with two layers of 100% cotton cheesecloth; discard bay leaves and herbs. Skim fat; return broth to Dutch oven.
3. Stir chopped meat, carrots, celery, and orzo into Dutch oven. Return to boiling; reduce heat. Simmer, covered, about 15 minutes or until vegetables and orzo are tender. Stir in spinach. Cook for 1 to 2 minutes more or just until fresh spinach is wilted or frozen spinach is heated through.
4. To serve, ladle soup into bowls. If desired, sprinkle individual servings with Parmesan cheese.
PER SERVING: 193 cal., 3 g total fat (1 g sat. fat), 53 mg chol., 487 mg sodium, 20 g carb., 2 g fiber, 22 g pro. Exchanges: 1 vegetable, 1 starch, 2 lean meat. Carb choices: 1.

Shrimp
Chowder

cook onion and garlic in hot oil over medium heat for 12 to 15 minutes or until onion is tender. Turn down heat as needed to prevent onion from overbrowning.

2. Stir in undrained tomatoes, broth, 1 cup *water*, the potatoes, Creole seasoning, red pepper, and hot pepper sauce. Bring to boiling; reduce heat. Simmer, covered, 15 to 20 minutes or until potatoes are just tender.

3. Meanwhile, in a medium bowl, beat cream cheese with an electric mixer on medium to high speed until smooth. Gradually beat in milk on low speed until mixture is very smooth.

4. Add cream cheese mixture, flounder, shrimp, and corn to soup. Return to boiling; reduce heat. Simmer, uncovered, for 3 to 5 minutes or until shrimp are opaque.

PER SERVING: 256 cal., 7 g total fat (2 g sat. fat), 87 mg chol., 599 mg sodium, 29 g carb., 4 g fiber, 21 g pro. Exchanges: 0.5 vegetable, 1.5 starch, 2.5 lean meat. Carb choices: 2.

Shrimp Chowder

Cream cheese adds richness to this tomatoey chowder.
SERVINGS 6 (about 1⅓ cups each)
CARB. PER SERVING 29 g

- 8 ounces fresh or frozen flounder fillets (about 2 medium fillets)
- 8 ounces fresh or frozen peeled and deveined medium shrimp
- 1 large onion, chopped (¾ cup)
- 2 cloves garlic, minced
- 1 tablespoon canola oil
- 1 14.5-ounce can diced tomatoes, undrained
- 1 14-ounce can vegetable broth or reduced-sodium chicken broth
- 12 ounces potatoes, scrubbed and cubed
- 1½ teaspoons Creole seasoning
- ⅛ to ¼ teaspoon crushed red pepper
  Bottled hot pepper sauce
- 3 ounces reduced-fat cream cheese (Neufchâtel), softened
- 1 cup fat-free milk
- 1½ cups frozen whole kernel corn

1. Thaw flounder and shrimp, if frozen. Rinse flounder and shrimp; pat dry with paper towels. Cut flounder into bite-size pieces. Set aside. In a 4- to 5-quart Dutch oven,

Weeknight Seafood Gumbo

Convenience products help you get this Southern-style stew to the table in 20 minutes or less.
SERVINGS 6 (scant 1 cup gumbo and ½ cup rice each)
CARB. PER SERVING 26 g

- 1 14.5-ounce can no-salt-added stewed tomatoes, undrained, cut up
- 1 10.75-ounce can condensed chicken gumbo soup
- 1 9-ounce package frozen cut okra (about 2 cups)
- 1 cup reduced-sodium chicken broth
- 1 8-ounce can whole oysters, drained
- 1 6.5-ounce can minced clams, drained
- 1 teaspoon dried thyme, crushed
- ½ teaspoon bottled hot pepper sauce
- 1¼ cups instant brown rice
- ¼ cup cooked turkey bacon pieces (about 4 slices)
  Fresh cilantro sprigs (optional)

1. In a large saucepan, combine undrained tomatoes, chicken gumbo soup, frozen okra, broth, oysters, clams, thyme, and hot pepper sauce. Bring to boiling; reduce heat. Simmer, uncovered, for 15 minutes.

2. Meanwhile, cook rice according to package directions. Stir cooked bacon pieces into gumbo mixture.

3. To serve, ladle gumbo mixture over rice in bowls. If desired, garnish with fresh cilantro.

PER SERVING: 193 cal., 3 g total fat (1 g sat. fat), 47 mg chol., 631 mg sodium, 26 g carb., 3 g fiber, 15 g pro. Exchanges: 1 vegetable, 1.5 starch, 1.5 lean meat. Carb choices: 2.

QUICK TIP ◗

Okra is a delicious and integral addition to classic gumbo—the trick is to not overcook it. Cooked for the suggested time, okra stays crisp-tender instead of turning mushy or slimy.

Weeknight Seafood Gumbo

sensational sandwiches

Yummy ingredients crowning a single bread plank, artfully arranged inside a bun, or filling a whole grain wrap—sandwiches are the perfect meals for on-the-go families. Best of all, these sandwiches are fun to make, easy to eat, and layered with healthful goodness.

Vinaigrette-Dressed Steak Sandwiches

Choose your favorite vinaigrette for this steak sandwich—any will do. A small amount is combined with mayonnaise for the sandwich spread. Fresh basil livens up the greens.

SERVINGS 4 (1 topped bread slice each)
CARB. PER SERVING 24 g

- 12 ounces boneless beef top sirloin steak, cut ½ inch thick
- ½ cup reduced-fat, reduced-calorie bottled balsamic-, raspberry-, or Italian-flavored vinaigrette
- ½ teaspoon crushed red pepper
- 1 clove garlic, minced
- ¼ cup light mayonnaise
- 1 small red onion, thinly sliced
- 2 teaspoons canola oil
- 4 ½-inch-thick slices hearty whole grain bread, toasted
- 1¼ cups small lettuce leaves
- ⅔ cup fresh basil leaves, thinly sliced

1. If desired, partially freeze steak for easier slicing. Trim fat from steak. Thinly slice steak across the grain into bite-size strips. In a medium bowl, combine vinaigrette, red pepper, and garlic. In a small bowl, combine 1 tablespoon of the vinaigrette mixture and the mayonnaise dressing; cover and chill.
2. Add steak strips to remaining vinaigrette mixture; stir to coat. Cover and marinate in the refrigerator for 1 hour. Drain steak strips; discard marinade.
3. In a large nonstick skillet, cook steak and onion in hot oil over medium-high heat for 2 to 3 minutes or until meat is browned and onion is crisp-tender.
4. To assemble, spread mayonnaise-vinaigrette mixture evenly onto one side of each bread slice. Top with lettuce and basil. With a slotted spoon, divide steak and onion mixture among the bread slices.

PER SERVING: 311 cal., 13 g total fat (2 g sat. fat), 41 mg chol., 553 mg sodium, 24 g carb., 5 g fiber, 25 g pro. Exchanges: 1 vegetable, 1 starch, 3 lean meat, 1.5 fat. Carb choices: 1.5.

Bagel Beef Sandwiches

*If you have your grill going for another meal,
toss on an extra steak. These stacked sandwiches are just
as delish when made with chilled beef.*

SERVINGS 4 (1 topped bagel half each)

CARB. PER SERVING 29 g

- ¼ cup sliced dried tomatoes (not oil-pack)
- 2 teaspoons olive oil
- 1 small red onion, sliced
- 12 ounces boneless beef sirloin steak, cut ¾ inch thick
- ¼ teaspoon garlic salt
- ¼ teaspoon black pepper
- 2 small whole wheat bagels, split and toasted (3 to 4 ounces total)
- 2 tablespoons light mayonnaise
- 1 tablespoon yellow mustard
- 2 cups mixed salad greens

1. Preheat broiler. Place tomatoes in a small bowl; cover with water. Microwave on 100% power (high) for 1 minute. Let stand 15 minutes.

2. Meanwhile, brush oil on onion slices. Arrange steak and onions on the unheated rack of a broiler pan; sprinkle with garlic salt and pepper. Broil 3 to 4 inches from heat for 12 to 16 minutes or until desired doneness, turning once. Thinly slice beef across the grain into bite-size pieces.

3. Meanwhile, drain tomatoes. Finely chop tomatoes. In a small bowl, combine tomatoes, mayonnaise, and mustard. Place each bagel half on a serving plate. Top bagel halves with steak, greens, onion, and mayonnaise mixture.

PER SERVING: 297 cal., 9 g total fat (2 g sat. fat), 38 mg chol., 295 mg sodium, 29 g carb., 4 g fiber, 25 g pro. Exchanges: 1 vegetable, 1.5 starch, 3 lean meat, 0.5 fat. Carb choices: 2.

Five-Spice Steak Wraps

*These wraps unite Asian and Mexican cuisines
into one freshly fused dish.*

SERVINGS 4 (1 wrap each)

CARB. PER SERVING 20 g

- 12 ounces boneless beef round steak
- 2 cups packaged shredded cabbage with carrot (coleslaw mix)
- ¼ cup red and/or green sweet pepper cut into thin bite-size strips
- ¼ cup carrot cut into thin bite-size strips
- ¼ cup snipped fresh chives
- 2 tablespoons rice vinegar
- ½ teaspoon toasted sesame oil
- ½ teaspoon five-spice powder
- ¼ teaspoon salt
- ¼ cup plain low-fat yogurt or light sour cream
- 4 8-inch flour tortillas

1. If desired, partially freeze steak for easier slicing. In a medium bowl, combine coleslaw mix, sweet pepper, carrot, and chives. In a small bowl, combine vinegar and sesame oil. Pour vinegar mixture over coleslaw mixture; toss to coat. Set aside.

2. Trim fat from steak. Thinly slice steak across the grain into bite-size strips. Sprinkle steak with five-spice powder and salt. Coat an unheated large nonstick skillet with *nonstick cooking spray*. Preheat over medium-high heat. Add steak strips; stir-fry for 3 to 4 minutes or until browned.

3. To assemble, spread 1 tablespoon of the yogurt down the center of each tortilla. Top with steak strips. Stir coleslaw mixture; spoon over steak. Fold in sides of tortillas. If desired, secure with wooden toothpicks.

PER SERVING: 237 cal., 7 g total fat (2 g sat. fat), 51 mg chol., 329 mg sodium, 20 g carb., 2 g fiber, 22 g pro. Exchanges: 1 vegetable, 1 starch, 2 medium-fat meat. Carb choices: 1..

Five-Spice
Steak Wraps

Bagel Beef
Sandwiches

Top 'Em

Sandwiches are a great way to sneak more veggies into your diet. Turn an ordinary cold-meat sandwich into extraordinary by adding one, two, or a few of these smart toppers.

1. **Fresh baby spinach leaves** or shredded regular spinach leaves.

2. **Assorted baby lettuces** or other salad greens.

3. **Red or yellow** tomato slices.

4. **Roasted red** sweet pepper pieces.

5. **Crunchy cucumber** sticks or slices.

6. **Packaged shredded cabbage** with carrot (coleslaw mix).

7. **Red onion** slices.

8. **Yellow, red, orange, or green** sweet pepper slices.

9. **Julienned or** coarsely shredded carrots.

10. **Packaged shredded broccoli** (broccoli slaw mix).

Grilled Beef and Avocado Pitas

Switch out lemon peel and juice for lime peel and juice for a different, but just as tasty, citrus flavor.

SERVINGS 6 (1 filled pita half each)
CARB. PER SERVING 24 g

- 12 ounces beef flank steak
- ½ cup bottled light clear Italian salad dressing
- ½ teaspoon finely shredded lime peel
- ¼ cup lime juice
- 2 tablespoons snipped fresh cilantro
- ¼ cup finely chopped onion
- ¼ teaspoon salt
- ¼ teaspoon black pepper
- 4 cups spring baby salad greens
- 1 medium red sweet pepper, cut into bite-size strips
- 1 medium avocado, halved, seeded, peeled, and thinly sliced
- 3 whole wheat pita bread rounds, halved

1. Score both sides of steak in a diamond pattern by making shallow diagonal cuts at 1-inch intervals. Place steak in a resealable plastic bag set in a shallow dish.

2. In a screw-top jar, combine salad dressing, lime peel, lime juice, and cilantro. Cover and shake well. Pour half of the salad dressing mixture into a small bowl and add onion; cover and chill until serving time. Pour the remaining salad dressing mixture in jar over steak in bag. Seal bag; turn to coat steak. Marinate in the refrigerator for 24 hours, turning bag occasionally.

3. Drain beef, discarding marinade. Sprinkle beef with salt and black pepper. For a charcoal grill, place steak on the grill rack directly over medium coals. Grill, uncovered, for 17 to 21 minutes for medium doneness (160°F), turning once. (For a gas grill, preheat grill. Reduce heat to medium. Place steak on grill rack. Cover and grill as above.)

4. To serve, thinly slice beef across grain. In a large bowl, toss together beef, salad greens, sweet pepper, avocado, and reserved dressing mixture. Fill each pita half with beef mixture.

TO BROIL STEAK: Place steak on the unheated rack of a broiler pan. Broil 3 to 4 inches from heat for 15 to 18 minutes for medium doneness (160°F), turning once.

PER SERVING: 254 cal., 11 g total fat (3 g sat. fat), 23 mg chol., 425 mg sodium, 24 g carb., 5 g fiber, 17 g pro. Exchanges: 1 vegetable, 1 starch, 2 lean meat, 0.5 fat. Carb. choices: 1.5.

Whiskey Burgers

If you enjoy new flavor combinations, try this zesty burger. It showcases ground venison dressed up with coffee, cocoa powder, chili powder, and whiskey.

SERVINGS 4 (1 burger and bun each)
CARB. PER SERVING 30 g

- 2 **bulbs garlic**
- 2 **teaspoons olive oil**
- 1 **teaspoon instant coffee crystals**
- 1 **teaspoon unsweetened cocoa powder**
- ¾ **teaspoon chili powder**
- ¼ **teaspoon salt**
- 1 **tablespoon whiskey or water**
- 1 **pound ground venison**
- 4 **small whole wheat hamburger buns, split and toasted**
  Lettuce leaves (optional)
  Thin slices fresh jalapeño chile peppers (optional)
  Tomato slices (optional)
  Thin red onion slices (optional)
  Dill pickle slices (optional)

1. Slice off the top ¼ to ½ inch of each garlic bulb to expose the cloves. Remove the papery outer skins, leaving the cloves intact. Place each garlic bulb on a 6-inch square of heavy foil; drizzle bulbs with olive oil. Wrap foil up around bulbs; seal. For a charcoal grill, place garlic on the grill rack directly over medium coals. Grill, uncovered, about 25 minutes or until garlic is soft.

Whiskey Burgers

(For a gas grill, preheat grill. Reduce heat to medium. Place foil-wrapped garlic bulbs on grill rack over heat. Cover and grill as above.) Remove garlic from grill and cool slightly.

2. Meanwhile, in a medium bowl, combine coffee crystals, cocoa powder, chili powder, and salt. Stir in whiskey or water. Add venison; mix well. Shape into four ½-inch-thick patties.

3. For a charcoal grill, place patties on the greased grill rack directly over medium coals. Grill, uncovered, for 10 to 13 minutes or until an instant-read thermometer inserted into side of each patty registers 160°F, turning once. (For a gas grill, preheat grill. Reduce heat to medium. Place patties on grill rack over heat. Cover and grill as above.)

4. Meanwhile, squeeze garlic cloves from the skins into a small bowl. Mash garlic with a fork. Spread garlic on bun bottoms; add lettuce (if using) and grilled patties. If desired, top with chile peppers, tomato, red onion, and/or pickles. Add bun tops.

PER SERVING: 315 cal., 6 g total fat (1 g sat. fat), 96 mg chol., 422 mg sodium, 30 g carb., 3 g fiber, 32 g pro. Exchanges: 2 starch, 3.5 lean meat, 1 fat. Carb choices: 2.

For carb-smart buns, read the nutrition labels and select those that are lower in carbohydrate and higher in fiber.

Salsa Beef
Sandwiches

Salsa Beef Sandwiches

Bottled salsa and chili powder add lively flavor to these sloppy joe-style sandwiches without a lot of work.
SERVINGS 6 (⅓ cup meat mixture and 1 bun each)
CARB. PER SERVING 24 g

- 1   pound lean ground beef
- 1   cup bottled chunky salsa
- ¼   cup water
- 1½ teaspoons chili powder
- 6   whole wheat hamburger buns, split and toasted

1. In a large skillet, cook meat until browned. Drain off fat. Stir in salsa, water, and chili powder. Bring to boiling; reduce heat. Simmer, uncovered, for 5 to 10 minutes or until desired consistency is reached. Divide mixture among hamburger buns.
PER SERVING: 258 cal., 9 g total fat (3 g sat. fat), 49 mg chol., 493 mg sodium, 24 g carb., 2 g fiber, 19 g pro. Exchanges: 1.5 starch, 2.5 lean meat, 0.5 fat. Carb choices: 1.5.

Smoky-Sweet Pork Planks

Dates and smoky chipotle peppers take bottled barbecue sauce to a new taste level.

SERVINGS 8 (1 topped bread slice each)
CARB. PER SERVING 29 g

- 1½ pounds boneless pork top loin roast (single loin) or boneless pork blade roast
- 2 teaspoons cooking oil
- 1½ cups water
- ½ cup ketchup
- ½ cup bottled low-calorie barbecue sauce
- 2 medium red onions, chopped (1 cup)
- 1 stalk celery, chopped (½ cup)
- ¼ cup snipped pitted dates
- 2 tablespoons packed brown sugar
- 2 tablespoons finely chopped canned chipotle peppers in adobo sauce
- 1 teaspoon dry mustard
- 1 teaspoon bottled minced garlic or 2 cloves garlic, minced
- 8 1-inch slices bread
- 8 lettuce leaves (optional)

1. Trim fat from roast. In a large saucepan, brown roast on all sides in hot oil. Drain off fat. Add the water, ketchup, barbecue sauce, red onions, celery, dates, brown sugar, chipotle peppers, mustard, and garlic. Bring to boiling; reduce heat. Simmer, covered, for 1½ to 2 hours or until meat is fork-tender, stirring sauce occasionally.
2. Remove meat from sauce. Pour sauce into a large glass measure or bowl; set aside. Using two forks, pull meat apart into shreds. Skim fat from sauce, if necessary. Return meat to saucepan; stir in enough of the sauce to make desired consistency. Heat through.
3. If desired, top bread slices with lettuce leaves; spoon meat mixture onto lettuce or bread.
PER SERVING: 261 cal., 5 g total fat (1 g sat. fat), 53 mg chol., 610 mg sodium, 29 g carb., 2 g fiber, 22 g pro. Exchanges: 1 starch, 1 carb., 2.5 lean meat. Carb choices: 2.

BBQ Chicken Sandwiches

If you like spicy, use Monterey Jack cheese with peppers.
SERVINGS 4 (1 sandwich each)
CARB. PER SERVING 34 g

- 2 cups sliced cooked chicken breast, cut into strips
- 1 medium carrot, shredded
- ½ cup bottled barbecue sauce
- 4 whole wheat hamburger buns, split and toasted
- ½ cup shredded reduced-fat Monterey Jack cheese (2 ounces) (optional)
- Pickle slices (optional)

1. In a medium saucepan, heat the chicken, carrot, and barbecue sauce over medium heat until bubbly.
2. Spoon chicken mixture onto bottom halves of buns. If desired, top chicken mixture with cheese. Place on a baking sheet. Broil 3 to 4 inches from heat for 1 to 2 minutes or until cheese melts. If desired, top with pickle slices. Add bun tops.
PER SERVING: 279 cal., 4 g total fat (1 g sat. fat), 60 mg chol., 622 mg sodium, 34 g carb., 3 g fiber, 26 g pro. Exchanges: 2 starch, 3 lean meat. Carb choices: 2.

Smoky-Sweet Pork Planks

Asian Chicken Wraps

Grab three prepared ingredients and a few fresh sweet pepper strips for a fast-fixin' meal.

SERVINGS 4 (1 wrap each)
CARB. PER SERVING 21 g

- 2 6-ounce cans no-salt-added chicken breast, drained
- ⅓ cup bottled reduced-calorie Asian sesame-ginger salad dressing
- 4 7- to 8-inch whole wheat flour tortillas
- 1 small red or green sweet pepper, cut into thin strips

1. In a medium bowl, stir together chicken and dressing. Divide mixture among tortillas. Top with pepper strips and roll up tortillas.

PER SERVING: 260 cal., 8 g total fat (2 g sat. fat), 60 mg chol., 618 mg sodium, 21 g carb., 11 g fiber, 25 g pro. Exchanges: 1.5 starch, 3 lean meat. Carb choices: 1.5.

Cheesy Chicken Sandwiches

To keep the tiny chicken pieces from sticking together, separate them with your fingers as you add them to the skillet and stir with a spoon as they cook.

SERVINGS 6 (1 sandwich each)
CARB. PER SERVING 33 g

- 2 skinless, boneless chicken breast halves, finely chopped (10 to 12 ounces total)
- 1 tablespoon canola oil
- 1 teaspoon chili powder
- ½ teaspoon ground cumin
- 1 clove garlic, minced
- Cayenne pepper
- ½ cup shredded reduced-fat sharp cheddar cheese (2 ounces)
- ¼ cup tub-style light cream cheese
- ¼ cup light sour cream
- 1 10-ounce can diced tomatoes and green chile peppers, drained
- 2 green onions, thinly sliced
- 2 tablespoons snipped fresh cilantro
- 12 slices white whole grain sandwich bread, crusts removed, or six 8-inch flour tortillas
- Cucumber slices, avocado slices, or tomato slices (optional)
- 12 leaves Bibb or green leaf lettuce

Italian Turkey Sandwiches

1. In a large skillet, cook chicken in hot oil until lightly browned and no longer pink. Stir in chili powder, cumin, garlic, and cayenne pepper; cook for 1 minute more. Cool slightly.

2. In a medium bowl, use a mixer to beat cheddar cheese, cream cheese, and sour cream until creamy and combined. Fold in chicken mixture, drained tomatoes and peppers, green onions, and cilantro. Cover and chill for up to 24 hours.

3. Spread mixture on half of the bread slices. If desired, top with cucumber, avocado, or tomato slices; add lettuce and remaining bread slices. (Or spread chicken mixture evenly over tortillas; top with lettuce and cucumber, avocado, or tomato slices. Roll up tortillas.)

PER SERVING: 300 cal., 9 g total fat (4 g sat. fat), 45 mg chol., 624 mg sodium, 33 g carb., 3 g fiber, 21 g pro. Exchanges: 1 vegetable, 2 starch, 2 lean meat, 0.5 fat. Carb choices: 2.

Italian Turkey Sandwiches

Fresh basil is the key here; dried simply doesn't work.

SERVINGS 4 (1 sandwich each)
CARB. PER SERVING 39 g

- ⅓ cup fine dry bread crumbs
- 2 teaspoons dried Italian seasoning, crushed
- 2 turkey tenderloins (about 1 pound total)
- 2 teaspoons olive oil
- 2 tablespoons snipped fresh basil
- 3 tablespoons light mayonnaise or salad dressing
- 8 ½-inch slices Italian bread, toasted

1 cup bottled roasted red and/or yellow sweet peppers,
cut into thin strips
Fresh basil leaves (optional)

1. In a large resealable plastic bag, combine the bread
crumbs and Italian seasoning. Split each turkey
tenderloin in half horizontally to make four $\frac{1}{2}$-inch
steaks. Place a turkey tenderloin steak in the bag; seal
and shake to coat. Repeat with remaining steaks.
2. In a very large nonstick skillet, cook steaks in hot oil
over medium heat about 10 minutes or until tender and
no longer pink (170°F), turning once.
3. In a small bowl, stir 1 tablespoon of the snipped basil
into the mayonnaise. Spread mixture on one side of half
of the bread slices. Top bread slices with turkey steaks,
sweet pepper strips, and the remaining snipped basil. If
desired, garnish with basil leaves. Top with remaining
bread slices.
PER SERVING: 384 cal., 9 g total fat (2 g sat. fat), 74 mg chol.,
522 mg sodium, 39 g carb., 3 g fiber, 35 g pro. Exchanges:
0.5 vegetable, 2.5 starch, 4 lean meat. Carb choices: 2.5.

Touchdown Tortilla Wraps

*Wrap these yummy meat-and-cheese rolls individually in
plastic wrap and pack in a cooler to tote to a tailgate party.*
SERVINGS 4 (1 wrap each)
CARB. PER SERVING 18 g

4   7- or 8-inch whole wheat tortillas
$\frac{1}{4}$ cup tub-style light cream cheese with chive and onion or
roasted garlic
16   fresh basil leaves
$\frac{1}{2}$ of a 7-ounce jar roasted red sweet peppers, well drained
and cut into $\frac{1}{4}$-inch-wide strips
4   ounces lower-sodium thinly sliced cooked roast beef,
ham, and/or turkey

1. Spread each tortilla with cream cheese. Cover cream
cheese with a layer of basil leaves, leaving a 1-inch
border. Arrange roasted red peppers on basil leaves. Top
with sliced meat.
2. Roll up each tortilla tightly into a spiral. Cut each
tortilla roll in half crosswise.
PER SERVING: 200 cal., 7 g total fat (3 g sat. fat), 25 mg chol.,
586 mg sodium, 18 g carb., 10 g fiber, 15 g pro. Exchanges:
1 starch, 2 lean meat, 1 fat. Carb choices: 1.

QUICK TIP ◖
To make tortillas easy
to roll, place them
between paper
towels and microwave
on high (100% power)
about 10 seconds.

Touchdown
Tortilla Wraps

Inside-Out Turkey Tempters

For easy eating and handling, wrap each sandwich roll in waxed or parchment paper.

SERVINGS 4 (1 roll-up each)

CARB. PER SERVING 19 g

- 12 thin slices cooked turkey breast or turkey ham
- ½ cup tub-style light cream cheese
- ½ cup packaged fresh julienned carrots
- 4 bread-and-butter or dill pickle spears
- 2 purchased soft breadsticks (6 to 8 inches long), halved lengthwise
  Leaf lettuce (optional)

1. Overlap three turkey slices so meat is the same length as the breadsticks. Spread meat with 2 tablespoons cream cheese. Place 2 tablespoons of the carrots, 1 pickle spear, and 1 breadstick half on edge of turkey. Roll up so meat is wrapped around breadstick. If desired, roll 1 or 2 lettuce leaves around outside of sandwich. Repeat with remaining ingredients.

PER SERVING: 194 cal., 5 g total fat (3 g sat. fat), 49 mg chol., 395 mg sodium, 19 g carb., 1 g fiber, 18 g pro. Exchanges: 1 starch, 2 lean meat, 0.5 fat. Carb choices: 1.

Greek Fusion Burgers

These turkey burgers revved up with chipotle chile peppers in adobo sauce are ideal a diabetes meal plan. Ground turkey breast, light cream cheese, and reduced-fat cheddar cheese all help to keep calories and fat to a minimum.

SERVINGS 4 (1 burger and pita half each)

CARB. PER SERVING 22 g

- 1 pound ground turkey breast
- 2 teaspoons finely chopped canned chipotle chile peppers in adobo sauce
- 1 teaspoon dried oregano, crushed
- ¼ cup tub-style light cream cheese, softened
- ¼ cup shredded reduced-fat cheddar cheese
- 1 tablespoon finely chopped green onion
- ⅛ teaspoon salt
- 2 large whole wheat pita bread rounds, halved crosswise
- ½ of a medium cucumber, cut into thin bite-size strips
- 8 small slices tomato

Greek Fusion Burgers

1. In a medium bowl, combine turkey, 1 teaspoon of the chile peppers, and the oregano. Shape mixture into four ½-inch-thick oval patties.

2. For a charcoal grill, place patties on the grill rack directly over medium coals. Grill, uncovered, for 10 to 13 minutes or until an instant-read thermometer inserted into side of each patty registers 165°F, turning once halfway through grilling. (For a gas grill, preheat grill. Reduce heat to medium. Place patties on grill rack over heat. Cover and grill as above.)

3. Meanwhile, in a small bowl, combine the remaining 1 teaspoon chile peppers, the cream cheese, cheddar cheese, green onion, and salt.

4. Open cut sides of halved pita bread rounds to make pockets. Spread cream cheese mixture into pockets. Add cucumber, grilled patties, and tomato slices.

PER SERVING: 272 cal., 6 g total fat (3 g sat. fat), 58 mg chol., 473 mg sodium, 22 g carb., 3 g fiber, 33 g pro. Exchanges: 1 vegetable, 1 starch, 4 lean meat, 0.5 fat. Carb choices: 1.5.

Grilled Jamaican Jerk Fish Wraps

The colorful combo of fresh spinach, tomato, and mango complements the jerk-seasoned fish.

SERVINGS 4 (1 wrap each)
CARB. PER SERVING 23 g

- 1 pound fresh or frozen skinless flounder, cod, or sole fillets
- 1½ teaspoons Jamaican jerk seasoning
- 4 7- to 8-inch whole grain flour tortillas
- 2 cups packaged fresh baby spinach
- ¾ cup chopped seeded tomato
- ¾ cup chopped fresh mango or pineapple
- 2 tablespoons snipped fresh cilantro
- 1 tablespoon finely chopped seeded fresh jalapeño chile pepper*
- 1 tablespoon lime juice

1. Thaw fish, if frozen. Rinse fish; pat dry with paper towels. Sprinkle Jamaican jerk seasoning over both sides of each fish fillet; rub in with your fingers. Measure thickness of fish.

2. For a charcoal grill, place tortillas on the greased rack directly over medium coals. Grill, uncovered, for 1 minute or until bottoms of tortillas have grill marks. Remove from grill and set aside. Place fish on the grill rack directly over the coals. Grill fish, uncovered, for 4 to 6 minutes per ½-inch thickness or until fish flakes easily when tested with a fork, turning once halfway through grilling. (For a gas grill, preheat grill. Reduce heat to medium. Place tortillas on greased grill rack over heat. Cover and grill as above. Remove tortillas from the grill and add fish; cover and grill as above.) Coarsely flake the fish.

3. Meanwhile, in a medium bowl, toss together spinach, tomato, mango, cilantro, chile pepper, and lime juice.

4. To assemble, place tortillas, grill-mark sides down, on a flat work surface. Top each tortilla with some of the spinach mixture and flaked fish. Roll up tortillas to enclose filling. Cut each in half to serve.

*TEST KITCHEN TIP: Because chile peppers contain volatile oils that can burn your skin and eyes, avoid direct contract with them as much as possible. When working with chile peppers, wear plastic or rubber gloves. If your bare hands do touch the peppers, wash your hands and nails well with soap and warm water.

PER SERVING: 254 cal., 4 g total fat (1 g sat. fat), 48 mg chol., 509 mg sodium, 23 g carb., 11 g fiber, 29 g pro. Exchanges: 1 vegetable, 1 starch, 3.5 lean meat. Carb choices: 1.5.

Open-Face Barbecue Tilapia Sandwiches

Grilled fish nestled on a bed of crunchy coleslaw and capped off with a drizzle of barbecue sauce makes these diabetes-friendly sandwiches sure to please.

SERVINGS 4 (1 topped bread slice each)
CARB. PER SERVING 13 g

- 4 4- to 5-ounce fresh or frozen skinless tilapia or flounder fillets
-    Nonstick cooking spray
- 2 tablespoons light mayonnaise
- 2 teaspoons lemon juice
- 2 cups packaged shredded cabbage with carrot (coleslaw mix)
- 4 slices whole wheat bread, toasted
- 2 tablespoons bottled low-calorie barbecue sauce

1. Thaw fish, if frozen. Rinse fish; pat dry with paper towels. Measure thickness of fish. Lightly coat both sides of each fish fillet with nonstick cooking spray.
2. For a charcoal grill, place fish on the greased rack directly over medium coals. Grill, uncovered, for 4 to 6 minutes per ½-inch thickness or until fish flakes easily when tested with a fork. (For a gas grill, preheat

Open-Face Barbecue
Tilapia Sandwiches

grill. Reduce heat to medium. Place fish on greased grill rack over heat. Cover and grill as directed.)

3. In a medium bowl, stir together mayonnaise and lemon juice. Add cabbage; toss to coat.

4. To assemble, spoon cabbage mixture onto toasted bread slices. Top with fish fillets. Drizzle fish with barbecue sauce.

PER SERVING: 206 cal., 5 g total fat (1 g sat. fat), 59 mg chol., 339 mg sodium, 13 g carb., 2 g fiber, 26 g pro. Exchanges: 0.5 vegetable, 1 starch, 3 lean meat. Carb choices: 1.

Cannellini-Tuna Wraps

Cannellini-Tuna Wraps

The more mashed the beans are, the more the mixture will hold together.

SERVINGS 6 (1 wrap each)

CARB. PER SERVING 28 g

¼ cup finely chopped red onion
2 tablespoons lemon juice
⅛ teaspoon black pepper
1 tablespoon olive oil
1 15-ounce can no-salt-added cannellini beans (white kidney beans), rinsed and drained
12 ounces cooked tuna,* broken into chunks, or two 6-ounce cans low-sodium chunk white tuna, drained
1 cup cherry tomatoes, quartered
¼ cup snipped fresh parsley
6 8-inch whole wheat, tomato, or spinach flour tortillas
½ cup julienned carrot

1. In a small bowl, combine red onion, lemon juice, pepper, and dash *salt*. Whisk in olive oil; set aside.

2. In a large bowl, slightly mash beans. Add tuna, tomatoes, and parsley. Pour dressing over mixture; stir.

3. Divide mixture among tortillas. Top with carrot. Roll up tightly. Serve immediately or cover and chill for up to 6 hours.

*TEST KITCHEN TIP: Purchase 1 pound frozen tuna steaks, cut 1 inch thick. Thaw fish. Rinse fish; pat dry with paper towels. Place fish on the greased unheated rack of a broiler pan. Broil 4 inches from heat for 8 to 12 minutes or until fish begins to flake when tested with a fork, turning once halfway through broiling. Use right away or freeze for later use. Makes about 12 ounces cooked fish.

PER SERVING: 297 cal., 7 g total fat (1 g sat. fat), 33 mg chol., 402 mg sodium, 28 g carb., 14 g fiber, 29 g pro. Exchanges: 2 starch, 3 lean meat. Carb choices: 2.

Curried Tuna Sandwiches

The tuna salad can be made ahead and refrigerated until you are ready to assemble the sandwiches.

SERVINGS 4 (1 sandwich each)

CARB. PER SERVING 28 g

1½ cups creamy deli coleslaw
1 small tomato, seeded and chopped
1 teaspoon curry powder
1 6-ounce can tuna, drained and flaked
¼ cup chopped peanuts
4 ciabatta rolls, sliced horizontally
4 large butterhead (Bibb or Boston) lettuce leaves
Light sour cream dip with chives (optional)

1. In a medium bowl, stir together coleslaw, tomato, and curry powder. Fold in tuna and chopped peanuts.

2. To serve, spoon the tuna mixture into sliced ciabatta rolls and top with lettuce leaves. If desired, top with dip.

PER SERVING: 254 cal., 9 g total fat (2 g sat. fat), 21 mg chol., 434 mg sodium, 28 g carb., 3 g fiber, 17 g pro. Exchanges: 1 vegetable, 1.5 starch, 1.5 lean meat, 1 fat. Carb choices: 2.

Italian Beans with Pesto Lettuce Wraps

Canned beans are a real timesaver, but they are higher in sodium than cooked dried beans.

SERVINGS 6 (about ¾ cup bean mixture and 2 lettuce leaves each)
CARB. PER SERVING 33 g

- 1 14-ounce can reduced-sodium chicken broth or vegetable broth
- ¾ cup bulgur
- 1 medium red sweet pepper, chopped (¾ cup)
- ⅓ cup refrigerated basil pesto
- 2 green onions, thinly sliced (¼ cup)
- 2 tablespoons balsamic vinegar
- 2 cups cooked or canned red kidney beans, pinto beans, Christmas lima beans, and/or other white beans*
  Black pepper
- 12 Bibb lettuce leaves

1. In a large saucepan, combine broth and bulgur. Bring to boiling; reduce heat. Cover and simmer about 15 minutes or until bulgur is tender. Remove from heat. Stir in sweet pepper, pesto, green onions, and balsamic vinegar. Stir in beans. Season with black pepper. Transfer to an airtight storage container. Cover and chill for up to 3 days.

2. To serve, spoon bean mixture evenly into lettuce leaves. Roll up.

*TEST KITCHEN TIP: To cook dried beans, rinse ¾ cup dried beans. In a large saucepan, combine rinsed beans and 5 cups water. Bring to boiling; reduce heat. Simmer, uncovered, for 2 minutes. Remove from heat. Cover and let stand for 1 hour. Drain; rinse beans and return to saucepan. Add 5 cups fresh water. Bring to boiling; reduce heat. Simmer, covered, for 1¼ to 1½ hours or until beans are tender; drain.

PER SERVING: 251 cal., 10 g total fat (0 g sat. fat), 2 mg chol., 267 mg sodium, 33 g carb., 8 g fiber, 10 g pro. Exchanges: 1 vegetable, 1.5 starch, 1 lean meat, 1.5 fat. Carb choices: 2.

Cheesy Eggplant Burgers

Looking for a change of pace from ordinary burgers? These grilled eggplant slices topped with smoky Gouda cheese and herb-seasoned tomatoes are the ticket.

SERVINGS 6 (1 burger and bread slice each)
CARB. PER SERVING 19 g

- 1 teaspoon garlic powder
- ½ teaspoon black pepper
- ⅛ teaspoon salt
- ½ cup chopped, seeded tomatoes
- 2 tablespoons olive oil
- 1 tablespoon snipped fresh oregano
- 2 teaspoons snipped fresh thyme
- 2 teaspoons cider vinegar
- 6 ½-inch-thick slices eggplant
- 6 ¾-ounce slices smoked Gouda cheese
- 6 ½-inch-thick slices whole grain baguette-style bread, toasted

1. In a small bowl, combine garlic powder, pepper, and salt. In another small bowl, combine half of the garlic powder mixture, the tomatoes, 1 tablespoon of the oil, the oregano, thyme, and vinegar. Set aside.

2. Brush the eggplant slices with the remaining 1 tablespoon oil and sprinkle with the remaining garlic powder mixture.

3. For a charcoal grill, place eggplant slices on the grill rack directly over medium coals. Grill, uncovered, for 6 to 8 minutes or just until tender and golden brown, turning once halfway through grilling and topping with the cheese slices for the last 2 minutes of grilling. (For a gas grill, preheat grill. Reduce heat to medium. Place eggplant slices on grill rack over heat. Cover and grill as above, topping with cheese as directed.)

4. Place eggplant slices on top of toasted bread slices. Top with tomato mixture.

PER SERVING: 201 cal., 11 g total fat (4 g sat. fat), 17 mg chol., 506 mg sodium, 19 g carb., 4 g fiber, 7 g pro. Exchanges: 1 vegetable, 1 starch, 0.5 high-fat meat, 1 fat. Carb choices: 1.

Italian Beans with Pesto Lettuce Wraps

Nutritious Wraps

With their perfect cup shape, Bibb lettuce leaves make great low-carb wraps. Try one of these tasty fillings nestled inside.

1. **A spoonful** of tabbouleh salad.
2. **Diced avocado,** shredded chicken, and a drizzle of spicy salsa.
3. **Assorted vegetable crudites** and a spoonful of blue cheese salad dressing.
4. **Hummus,** sliced cucumber, and crumbled feta cheese.
5. **Chilled** leftover stir-fry.
6. **Flaked canned tuna,** thin slices red onion, and halved grape tomatoes.
7. **Pulled roasted turkey,** shredded carrots and cucumbers, and a drizzle of ranch salad dressing.

Cheesy Eggplant Burgers

Tomato-Edamame
Grilled Cheese

Tomato-Edamame Grilled Cheese

*Shelled edamame (eh-dah-MAH-meh) beans
look like small limas, and their delicate flavor is a cross
between a mild nut and a sweet pea. The leftover
soybean spread makes a great dip for crisp fresh veggies.
To store, tightly cover and refrigerate for up to three days.*

SERVINGS 4 (1 sandwich each)

CARB. PER SERVING 21 g

- 1 bulb garlic
- 1 teaspoon canola oil
- 1 12-ounce package frozen shelled sweet soybeans (edamame)
- ¼ cup lemon juice
- ¼ cup water
- ½ teaspoon salt
- ½ teaspoon ground cumin
- ⅓ cup snipped fresh Italian (flat-leaf) parsley
- 8 very thin slices firm-texture whole wheat bread
- 4 ounces reduced-fat Monterey Jack cheese, cut into 4 slices
- 1 medium tomato, thinly sliced

1. For soybean spread: Preheat oven to 425°F. Slice off top ½ inch of garlic bulb. Remove papery outer skins, leaving cloves intact. Place bulb, cut side up, in custard cup. Drizzle with oil; cover with foil. Roast about 15 minutes or until soft. Cool.

2. Meanwhile, cook soybeans according to package directions. Drain; rinse with cold water.

3. Squeeze 3 garlic cloves from bulb and place in a food processor. (Wrap and refrigerate remaining garlic cloves for another use.) Add cooled soybeans, lemon juice, the water, the salt, and cumin to garlic in food processor. Cover and process until smooth. Transfer to a small bowl. Stir in parsley.

4. For sandwiches: Spread one side of each bread slice with 2 tablespoons soybean mixture. Top spread sides of 4 bread slices with a cheese slice and tomato slices. Top with remaining bread slices, spread sides down.

5. Place sandwiches on a nonstick griddle or nonstick extra-large skillet over medium to medium-high heat. Cook for 5 to 6 minutes or until golden and cheese is melted, turning once.

PER SERVING: 226 cal., 10 g total fat (4 g sat. fat), 20 mg chol., 619 mg sodium, 21 g carb., 5 g fiber, 15 g pro. Exchanges: 1.5 starch, 2 lean meat, 0.5 fat. Carb choices: 1.5.

Nutty Cucumber Sandwiches

*Select chèvre that has been rolled in cracked black pepper
to add another flavor dimension to this sandwich.*

SERVINGS 4 (1 sandwich each)

CARB. PER SERVING 36 g

- ½ cup fresh snow pea pods, trimmed
- ½ of a medium cucumber
- 8 thin slices rye bread
- 3 to 4 ounces soft goat cheese (chèvre)
- ⅓ cup seasoned roasted soy nuts (such as ranch or garlic)
- 1 medium tomato, thinly sliced
- Salt

1. In a small saucepan, cook the pea pods in lightly salted boiling water for 2 minutes. Drain; rinse with cold water. Drain again. Place pea pods in a small bowl; chill.

2. Use a vegetable peeler to remove a few lengthwise strips of peel from cucumber. Thinly slice cucumber.

3. Spread one side of each bread slice with goat cheese. Sprinkle 4 bread slices with soy nuts, gently pressing nuts into the cheese. Top with cucumber slices, tomato slices, and pea pods. Sprinkle with salt. Top with remaining bread slices.

PER SERVING: 276 cal., 9 g total fat (4 g sat. fat), 10 mg chol., 540 mg sodium, 36 g carb., 6 g fiber, 14 g pro. Exchanges: 1 vegetable, 2 starch, 1 medium-fat meat. Carb choices: 2.5.

QUICK TIP

Keep the wrap on the roll by securing a strip of parchment or waxed paper with a wooden toothpick around each sandwich. Simply slide down the paper strip as you eat your way to the bottom.

All-Wrapped-Up Salad

Using whole grain tortillas helps boost the fiber in this fresh-tasting wrap.

SERVINGS 2 (1 wrap each)
CARB. PER SERVING 20 g

- 2 8-inch whole grain, whole wheat, or flour tortillas
- ¾ cup shredded romaine and/or fresh spinach
- ½ of an avocado, halved, seeded, peeled, and sliced
- ¼ of a cucumber, halved lengthwise, seeded, and thinly sliced
- ¼ cup shredded Monterey Jack cheese with jalapeño peppers (1 ounce)

  Purchased salsa (optional)

1. On each tortilla, layer romaine, avocado, cucumber, and cheese. Roll up tightly. If desired, halve tortillas diagonally. Wrap each tightly with plastic wrap. Chill for up to 6 hours.

2. If desired, serve with salsa.

PER SERVING: 248 cal., 13 g total fat (4 g sat. fat), 13 mg chol., 401 mg sodium, 20 g carb., 12 g fiber, 13 g pro. Exchanges: 0.5 vegetable, 1 starch, 1 high-fat meat, 1 fat. Carb choices: 1.

All-Wrapped-Up Salad

simple sides
and salads

Make a nutritious family meal by using one of these vibrant recipes with simply roasted, grilled, or pan-seared poultry, fish, or meat. Each colorful side dish bursts with fresh flavor and lots of vitamins and other healthful nutrients. Complete your meal plan with a veggie-filled side that fits your fat and carb requirements.

Tomato-Pepper Salad

Sweet peppers come in a variety of colors, including yellow, green, orange, red, and purple. If you like, mix and match the hues of the peppers you use in this salad for eye-catching contrast.

SERVINGS 8 (about ¾ cup each)
CARB. PER SERVING 7 g

3 large yellow sweet peppers, thinly sliced into rings
3 or 4 medium tomatoes (about 1 pound)
⅓ cup crumbled reduced-fat blue cheese
1 recipe Herb-Dijon Vinaigrette (below)
Fresh watercress or spinach leaves (optional)

1. In a covered large skillet, cook sweet pepper rings in boiling water for 1 to 2 minutes or just until crisp-tender. Drain and cool. Cover and chill for 1 to 24 hours.
2. To serve, cut tomatoes into wedges. On a platter, arrange tomato wedges and pepper rings. Top with cheese. Shake dressing to mix; drizzle onto salad. If desired, garnish with watercress.*

HERB-DIJON VINAIGRETTE: In a screw-top jar, combine 2 tablespoons olive oil, 2 tablespoons white wine vinegar or balsamic vinegar, 1 tablespoon snipped fresh chives, 2 teaspoons snipped fresh basil, 1 teaspoon sugar, ½ teaspoon Dijon-style mustard, and ⅛ teaspoon black pepper. Cover and shake well to mix; chill for up to 3 days.

*TEST KITCHEN TIP: To tote this salad, pack pepper rings, tomatoes, cheese, Herb-Dijon Vinaigrette, and watercress (if using) in separate containers in an insulated cooler with ice packs. Assemble at the site.

PER SERVING: 76 cal., 4 g total fat (1 g sat. fat), 2 mg chol., 74 mg sodium, 7 g carb., 1 g fiber, 2 g pro. Exchanges: 1.5 vegetable, 1 fat. Carb choices: 0.5.

Tomato and
Red Onion Salad

Triple-Green Bean Salad

QUICK TIP ◖

A quick plunge in icy-cold water stops the cooking process and helps keep the beans vibrant green.

Tomato and Red Onion Salad

Choose heirloom and cherry tomatoes in a variety of colors. If desired, halve the cherry tomatoes or leave some whole.

SERVINGS 6 to 8 (1⅓ cups to 1 cup each)

CARB. PER SERVING 19 g or 12 g

- 1 medium red onion, cut into ¼-inch slices
- ½ cup cider vinegar
- ¼ cup sugar*
- 8 cups cut-up tomatoes (about 3 pounds)

1. In a medium bowl, combine 4 cups ice-cold *water* and 1 teaspoon *salt*; stir to dissolve salt. Add onion slices; stir to separate rings. Let stand for 20 minutes; drain.

2. Meanwhile, for dressing: In a small bowl, whisk together vinegar, sugar, and ½ teaspoon each *salt* and *black pepper*. In an extra-large bowl, combine tomatoes and drained onions. Add dressing; gently toss to coat. Let stand for 5 minutes.

***SUGAR SUBSTITUTES:** Choose from Splenda granular, Equal Spoonful or packets, or Sweet'N Low bulk or packets. Follow package directions to use product amount equivalent to ¼ cup sugar.

PER SERVING: 85 cal., 0 g total fat, 0 mg chol., 304 mg sodium, 19 g carb., 3 g fiber, 2 g pro. Exchanges: 1.5 vegetable, 1 carb. Carb choices: 1.

PER SERVING WITH SUBSTITUTE: Same as above, except 57 cal., 12 g carb. Exchanges: 0.5 carb.

Triple-Green Bean Salad

When the farmer's market tables are overflowing with beans, pick up a mix of green and yellow wax beans.

SERVINGS 4 to 6 (1 cup to scant ¾ cup each)

CARB. PER SERVING 8 g

- 12 ounces fresh green beans, ends trimmed if desired
- 2 tablespoons water
- ⅓ cup fresh parsley, coarsely chopped
- 4 green onions, sliced (green tops only)
- 2 stalks celery, cut into ½-inch slices
- 2 tablespoons olive oil
- 2 tablespoons lime juice
- ¼ teaspoon sea salt or salt
  Lime wedges (optional)

1. In a 1½- or 2-quart microwave-safe casserole, combine green beans and water. Cover and microwave on high (100% power) for 5 to 7 minutes or just until tender, stirring once after 3 minutes. Drain in a colander. Rinse with cold water; drain again. Transfer to a serving dish. Toss with parsley, green onion tops, celery, oil, and lime juice. Cover and let stand for up to 30 minutes.

2. Sprinkle with salt just before serving. If desired, squeeze lime wedges over individual servings.

PER SERVING: 98 cal., 7 g total fat (1 g sat. fat), 0 mg chol., 127 mg sodium, 8 g carb., 4 g fiber, 2 g pro. Exchanges: 1.5 vegetable, 1.5 fat. Carb choices: 0.5.

New Potato Salad

No warm-weather picnic or potluck is complete without potato salad. This carb-conscious new potato version is the perfect serve-along for burgers, chicken, or just about any other grilled summer favorite.

SERVINGS 16 (½ cup each)

CARB. PER SERVING 14 g

2 pounds tiny new potatoes
1 cup low-fat mayonnaise dressing or light salad dressing
2 stalks celery, chopped (1 cup)
1 large onion, chopped (¾ cup)
⅓ cup chopped sweet or dill pickles
½ teaspoon salt
¼ teaspoon coarsely ground black pepper
2 hard-cooked eggs, chopped
1 to 2 tablespoons fat-free milk
Coarsely ground black pepper

1. In a large saucepan, combine potatoes and enough water to cover potatoes. Bring to boiling; reduce heat. Cover and simmer for 15 to 20 minutes or just until tender. Drain well; cool potatoes. Cut potatoes into quarters.

2. In a large bowl, combine mayonnaise dressing, celery, onion, pickles, salt, and the ¼ teaspoon pepper. Add the potatoes and eggs, gently tossing to coat. Cover and chill for 6 to 24 hours.

3. To serve, stir enough of the milk into salad to reach desired consistency. Season to taste with additional pepper.

PER SERVING: 86 cal., 3 g total fat (1 g sat. fat), 27 mg chol., 254 mg sodium, 14 g carb., 1 g fiber, 2 g pro. Exchanges: 1 starch, 0.5 fat. Carb choices: 1.

Cilantro Three-Bean Salad

Forget old-fashioned three-bean salad! Try this snazzy version that features garbanzo beans, small white beans, and baby limas fired up with jalapeño or serrano peppers and seasoned with cilantro and a low-carb dressing that uses only 2 teaspoons of brown sugar.

SERVINGS 14 (½ cup each)

CARB. PER SERVING 16 g

½ cup cider vinegar
3 tablespoons salad oil
2 teaspoons packed brown sugar
¼ teaspoon salt
¼ teaspoon black pepper
1 15-ounce can garbanzo beans (chickpeas), rinsed and drained
1 15-ounce can small white beans, rinsed and drained
1 10-ounce package frozen baby lima beans, thawed
3 medium carrots, coarsely chopped
⅓ cup snipped fresh cilantro
1 to 2 fresh jalapeño or serrano chile peppers, seeded and finely chopped*
Snipped fresh cilantro (optional)

1. For dressing: In a large bowl, whisk together cider vinegar, oil, brown sugar, salt, and black pepper. Stir in garbanzo beans, white beans, lima beans, carrots, the ⅓ cup snipped cilantro, and the chile peppers. Cover and chill for 2 to 24 hours, stirring occasionally.

2. Transfer bean mixture to a serving bowl. If desired, garnish with additional snipped cilantro.**

*****TEST KITCHEN TIP:** Because chile peppers contain volatile oils that can burn your skin and eyes, avoid direct contact with them as much as possible. When working with chile peppers, wear plastic or rubber gloves. If your bare hands do touch the peppers, wash your hands and nails well with soap and warm water.

******TEST KITCHEN TIP:** To tote, place salad in an insulated container with ice packs.

PER SERVING: 107 cal., 3 g total fat (0 g sat. fat), 0 mg chol., 205 mg sodium, 16 g carb., 4 g fiber, 5 g pro. Exchanges: 1 starch, 0.5 fat. Carb choices: 1.

Orange-Asparagus Salad
recipe on page 99

New Potato Salad

Cilantro Three-Bean Salad

Power Up

Take steps to eat better by adding these five diabetes power foods into your meal plan.

1. **Asparagus:** High in fiber, the B vitamin folate, and a health-promoting antioxidant called glutathione.

2. **Beans (legumes):** High in fiber and protein and a good source of vitamins and minerals, such as folate, iron, magnesium, and potassium.

3. **Broccoli:** High in vitamin C and a good source of fiber and the antioxidant beta-carotene, which the body uses to make vitamin A.

4. **Carrots:** Provide vitamin A from the antioxidant beta-carotene. And they are another source of fiber and heart-healthy flavonoids.

5. **Spinach:** Loaded with vitamins and minerals, including vitamins B2 and B6, folate, copper, magnesium, potassium, zinc, and fiber.

Southwest Pasta Salad

Your family will enjoy eating veggies with this scrumptious dish that showcases multigrain pasta teamed with five vegetables and a spinach pesto.

SERVINGS 6 to 8 (⅔ cup to ½ cup each)

CARB. PER SERVING 18 g

- 4 ounces dried multigrain penne pasta (1¼ cups)
- ½ cup thin bite-size strips jicama
- ½ cup thin bite-size strips zucchini
- ½ cup chopped green or red sweet pepper
- ¼ cup frozen whole kernel corn, thawed and drained
- ¼ cup sliced radishes
- 1 recipe Creamy Spinach Pesto (right)

1. Cook pasta according to package directions. Drain pasta and rinse with cold water; drain again. Transfer pasta to a large bowl. Add jicama, zucchini, sweet pepper, corn, and radishes. Add Creamy Spinach Pesto; toss gently to coat.

2. Serve immediately or cover and chill for up to 24 hours. If chilled, stir before serving.

CREAMY SPINACH PESTO: In a blender or food processor, combine 1¼ cups lightly packed fresh spinach, ½ cup lightly packed fresh cilantro, 2 tablespoons toasted sliced almonds, 2 tablespoons water, 1 tablespoon canola oil or olive oil, ½ teaspoon salt, ⅛ to ¼ teaspoon crushed red pepper, and ⅛ teaspoon black pepper. Cover and blend or process until smooth. Add ¼ cup light sour cream. Cover and blend or process just until combined.

PER SERVING: 130 cal., 5 g total fat (1 g sat. fat), 3 mg chol., 219 mg sodium, 18 g carb., 3 g fiber, 5 g pro. Exchanges: 0.5 vegetable, 1 starch, 1 fat. Carb choices: 1.

Strawberry-Radish
Salad

Strawberry-Radish Salad

*When you want to serve a health-smart tossed salad,
make this delicious fat-free lemon salad dressing
and toss it with mixed salad greens.*

SERVINGS 6 (1 cup greens and ½ cup fruit
mixture each)

CARB. PER SERVING 23 g or 15 g

- 1 pint fresh strawberries, hulled and halved or quartered
- 2 oranges, peeled and sectioned
- 6 radishes, sliced paper thin
- 3 green onions, thinly bias-sliced
- 4 teaspoons lemon juice
- 1 tablespoon sugar*
- 1 5-ounce package mesclun greens
- 1 recipe No-Fat Lemon Vinaigrette (below)

1. In a medium bowl, combine strawberries, orange
sections, radishes, green onions, lemon juice, and sugar.
Let stand at room temperature for 10 to 15 minutes to
allow flavors to blend.

2. In a large bowl, toss the mesclun with the No-Fat
Lemon Vinaigrette. Arrange mesclun mixture on a
serving platter. Spoon strawberry mixture on top of
mesclun mixture.

NO-FAT LEMON VINAIGRETTE: In a small stainless-steel
saucepan, combine ⅓ cup finely chopped shallots,
¼ cup dry white wine, 3 tablespoons sugar or sugar
substitute* equivalent to 3 tablespoons sugar,
1 tablespoon rice vinegar, and 3 cloves garlic, minced.
Stir in 1 teaspoon cornstarch. Cook and stir until
mixture is slightly thickened and bubbly. Cook and stir
for 1 minute more; cool. Stir in 1 teaspoon finely
shredded lemon peel, ¼ cup lemon juice, ¼ teaspoon
salt, and ⅛ teaspoon black pepper.

*SUGAR SUBSTITUTES: Choose from Splenda granular or
Sweet'N Low bulk or packets. Follow package directions to
use product amount equivalent to 1 tablespoon and
3 tablespoons sugar.

PER SERVING: 91 cal., 0 g total fat, 0 mg chol., 111 mg sodium,
21 g carb., 3 g fiber, 2 g pro. Exchanges: 0.5 carb., 1 vegetable,
0.5 fruit. Carb choices: 1.5.

PER SERVING WITH SUBSTITUTE: Same as above, except 69 cal.,
15 g carb. Carb. choices: 1.

Orange-Asparagus Salad

*A tart-sweet citrus-and-mustard dressing brings out
the best in this delightful medley of garden-fresh asparagus
and juicy orange sections. Pictured on page 97.*

SERVINGS 2 (¾ cup each)

CARB. PER SERVING 8 g

- 8 ounces fresh asparagus spears
- 2 tablespoons orange juice
- 2 teaspoons olive oil
- ½ teaspoon Dijon-style mustard
- ⅛ teaspoon salt
-   Black pepper
- 1 medium orange, peeled and sectioned

1. Snap off and discard woody bases from asparagus. If
desired, scrape off scales. Cut stems into 2-inch-long
pieces. In a covered small saucepan, cook asparagus in
a small amount of boiling water for 1 minute; drain.
Cool immediately in a bowl of ice water. Drain on
paper towels.

2. For dressing: In a medium bowl, whisk together
orange juice, oil, mustard, salt, and pepper. Add
asparagus and orange sections; stir gently to coat. Serve
immediately or cover and chill for up to 6 hours.

PER SERVING: 74 cal., 5 g total fat (1 g sat. fat), 0 mg chol.,
177 mg sodium, 8 g carb., 2 g fiber, 2 g pro. Exchanges:
1 vegetable, 1 fat. Carb choices: 0.5.

If you're short on time, grab a bag of shredded cabbage and carrots (coleslaw mix) to get you started. You can also stir the mix into vegetable stew, toss it in a salad, heap it on a sandwich, or roll it in a wrap.

Honey-Mustard
Fruit Slaw

Honey-Mustard Fruit Slaw

Traditional coleslaw gets a makeover with an added twist of apple or pear and homemade honey-mustard dressing. Slaw makes a great side dish for sandwiches.

SERVINGS 2 (³⁄₄ cup each)
CARB. PER SERVING 13 g

- ³⁄₄ cup shredded green cabbage
- ½ cup shredded carrot
- ⅓ cup coarsely chopped apple or pear
- 2 teaspoons salad oil
- 2 teaspoons Dijon-style mustard or coarse-grain brown mustard
- 1½ teaspoons lemon juice
- 1½ teaspoons honey
- 1 small clove garlic, minced
- 1 tablespoon chopped peanuts or cashews

1. In a medium bowl, toss together cabbage, carrot, and apple; set aside.

2. For dressing: In a small screw-top jar, combine salad oil, mustard, lemon juice, honey, and garlic. Cover and shake well. Pour dressing over cabbage mixture; toss gently to coat. Cover and refrigerate for 2 to 24 hours.

3. Before serving, sprinkle the cabbage mixture with chopped peanuts.

PER SERVING: 118 cal., 7 g total fat (1 g sat. fat), 0 mg chol., 181 mg sodium, 13 g carb., 2 g fiber, 2 g pro. Exchanges: 0.5 vegetable, 1 carb., 1 fat. Carb choices: 1.

Kohlrabi-Carrot Salad with Dill Vinaigrette

Choose small, well-shaped bulbs when you're shopping for kohlrabi. Bulbs larger than 3 inches in diameter tend to be woody.

SERVINGS 6 (²⁄₃ cup each)
CARB. PER SERVING 7 g

- 4 medium kohlrabi (about 1½ pounds total),* peeled and chopped (3 cups)
- 1 medium red and/or green sweet pepper, seeded and chopped (³⁄₄ cup)

Applesauce

Applesauce

For a smoother applesauce, process the apple mixture half at a time, in a food processor. The mixture will be slightly thinner in consistency, and the skin will be less noticeable.

SERVINGS 14 (about ½ cup each; 7½ pints total)
CARB. PER SERVING 25 g or 22 g

6   sprigs fresh thyme
4   pounds cooking apples, cored and cut into chunks
½   cup water
½   cup granulated sugar*
    Brown sugar (optional)
    Fresh thyme sprigs (optional)

1. Tie the 6 sprigs thyme with clean kitchen string. In an 8-quart Dutch oven, combine apples, tied thyme, and the water. Bring to boiling; reduce heat. Simmer, covered, about 20 minutes or until apples are just beginning to break up, stirring occasionally. Remove thyme. With a potato masher or large spoon, mash apples slightly. Stir in sugar.
2. Stir before serving. If desired, garnish with a sprinkle of brown sugar and fresh thyme. Or cool completely and ladle applesauce into half-pint freezer containers, leaving a ½-inch head space. Seal and label. Store for up to 3 weeks in the refrigerator or 6 months in the freezer.
SLOW COOKER METHOD: Place apple chunks in a 5- to 6-quart slow cooker. Stir in ½ cup granulated sugar* and 4 to 6 inches stick cinnamon (omit thyme and water). Cover; cook on high-heat setting for 3½ to 4 hours or until apples are very tender. Cool mixture about 1 hour. Remove cinnamon. Mash slightly with a potato masher or process with an immersion blender. Stir before serving.
TO FREEZE: Quick-cool applesauce by placing Dutch oven or slow cooker liner in a sink filled with ice water; stir mixture to cool. Ladle into wide-top freezer containers, leaving a ½-inch headspace. Seal, label, and freeze.
*****SUGAR SUBSTITUTES:** Choose from Splenda granular, Equal Spoonful or packets, or Sweet'N Low bulk or packets. Follow package directions to use product amount equivalent to ½ cup granulated sugar. If using the slow cooker method, do not choose Equal.
PER SERVING: 111 cal., 0 g total fat, 0 mg chol., 2 mg sodium, 29 g carb., 4 g fiber, 0 g pro. Exchanges: 1 fruit, 0.5 carb. Carb choices: 2.
PER SERVING WITH SUBSTITUTE: Same as above, except 83 cal., 22 g carb. Carb choices: 1.5.

1   medium carrot, chopped (½ cup)
½   of a small onion, chopped (¼ cup)
1   recipe Dill Vinaigrette (below)
6   lettuce leaves

1. In a large bowl, combine kohlrabi, sweet pepper, carrot, and onion. Add Dill Vinaigrette; toss gently to coat. Cover and chill for 2 hours, stirring occasionally to coat with dressing.
2. Stir before serving. Serve salad on lettuce leaves.
DILL VINAIGRETTE: In a small screw-top jar, combine ¼ cup cider vinegar, 2 teaspoons olive oil, 1 teaspoon sugar,** 1 teaspoon snipped fresh dill or ¼ teaspoon dried dill, ¼ teaspoon celery seeds, ⅛ teaspoon salt, and ⅛ teaspoon black pepper. Cover and shake well. Use immediately or cover and chill for up to 1 week.
*****TEST KITCHEN TIP:** If desired, substitute 3 cups chopped green cabbage (about 12 ounces) for the kohlrabi.
******SUGAR SUBSTITUTES:** Choose from Splenda granular, Equal Spoonful or packets, or Sweet'N Low bulk or packets. Follow package directions to use product amount equivalent to 1 teaspoon sugar.
MAKE-AHEAD DIRECTIONS: Prepare as directed in Step 1, except chill for up to 2 days. Serve as directed in Step 2.
PER SERVING: 48 cal., 2 g total fat (0 g sat. fat), 0 mg chol., 73 mg sodium, 7 g carb., 3 g fiber, 2 g pro. Exchanges: 1.5 vegetable. Carb choices: 0.5.
PER SERVING WITH SUBSTITUTE: Same as above, except 45 cal.

Five-Minute Pilaf

Brown rice that's dressed up with frozen veggies, reduced-fat pesto, and a sprinkling of nuts is an eye-catching and nutritious side dish to go with your favorite broiled or grilled meat, poultry, or fish.

SERVINGS 6 (½ cup each)
CARB. PER SERVING 17 g

- 1 8.8-ounce pouch cooked brown rice
- 2 cups frozen Italian-blend vegetables or frozen zucchini and yellow summer squash
- ¼ cup refrigerated reduced-fat basil pesto
- 2 tablespoons pine nuts or chopped walnuts, toasted

1. In a large microwave-safe bowl, combine brown rice and frozen vegetables. Cover bowl. Microwave on high (100% power) for 4 to 5 minutes or until vegetables are crisp-tender and mixture is heated through, stirring once or twice during cooking. Stir in pesto. To serve, sprinkle with pine nuts.

PER SERVING: 136 cal., 6 g total fat (1 g sat. fat), 3 mg chol., 110 mg sodium, 17 g carb., 2 g fiber, 4 g pro. Exchanges: 0.5 vegetable, 1 starch, 1 fat. Carb choices: 1.

Sesame Asparagus

Asparagus will stay fresh longer if you wrap the bases of the spears in a wet paper towel and keep them tightly sealed in a plastic bag in the refrigerator. The asparagus should last for up to four days.

SERVINGS 4 (about 5 spears each)
CARB. PER SERVING 4 g

- 1 pound fresh asparagus spears, trimmed
- 4 teaspoons reduced-sodium soy sauce

Five-Minute Pilaf

- ¼ teaspoon toasted sesame oil
  Sesame seeds, toasted

1. In a covered large saucepan, cook asparagus in boiling water for 1 minute. Using tongs, transfer asparagus to a large bowl of ice water. Let stand for 2 minutes. Drain well and pat dry with paper towels. Place asparagus in a large resealable plastic bag.
2. In a small bowl, whisk together soy sauce and sesame oil; pour over asparagus. Seal bag. Chill for 1 to 4 hours. Drain, discarding soy sauce mixture. To serve, sprinkle asparagus with sesame seeds.

PER SERVING: 28 cal., 1 g total fat (0 g sat. fat), 0 mg chol., 178 mg sodium, 4 g carb., 2 g fiber, 3 g pro. Exchanges: 1 vegetable. Carb choices: 0.

Grilled Vegetables with Vinaigrette

The sweet peppers in this Italian-inspired veggie mix are excellent sources of beta-carotene, which helps protect against heart disease.

SERVINGS 8 (1 cup each)
CARB. PER SERVING 10 g

- 1 pound fresh asparagus spears, trimmed
- 1 pound green and/or yellow pattypan squash, halved, and/or 1 pound zucchini and/or yellow summer squash, cut into 1-inch pieces
- 2 medium red and/or yellow sweet peppers, cut into ½-inch strips
- 2 cups red and/or yellow cherry tomatoes
- ¾ cup bottled light balsamic vinaigrette salad dressing
  Black pepper

1. In a very large bowl, combine asparagus, squash, sweet peppers, and tomatoes. Add balsamic vinaigrette; toss to coat. Cover and marinate in the refrigerator for 1 to 4 hours. Remove vegetables from vinaigrette, reserving vinaigrette.
2. Heat grill to medium and lightly oil rack. Place vegetables in a grill wok. Grill vegetables, stirring occasionally, for 8 to 10 minutes or until crisp-tender. If the vegetables appear dry while cooking, brush with some of the reserved vinaigrette.
3. To serve, arrange vegetables on a platter. Sprinkle with black pepper. Drizzle with reserved vinaigrette.

PER SERVING: 53 cal., 1 g total fat (0 g sat. fat), 0 mg chol., 223 mg sodium, 10 g carb., 3 g fiber, 2 g pro. Exchanges: 1.5 vegetable. Carb choices: 0.5.

Sesame Asparagus

▶ QUICK TIP
Make over leftovers into a main dish. Toss squash mixture with hot cooked whole grain spaghetti and a little lean protein, such as chicken.

Skillet Squash
Reap the benefits of an abundant summer squash crop with this vitamin-packed ratatouille-style dish.
SERVINGS 6 (²/₃ cup each)
CARB. PER SERVING 8 g

- 2 medium zucchini, chopped
- 2 medium yellow summer squash, chopped
- 1 medium onion, thinly sliced
- 2 teaspoons olive oil
- 1 4-ounce can diced green chiles, undrained
- 2 medium tomatoes, chopped
- 2 teaspoons snipped fresh oregano or ½ teaspoon dried oregano, crushed
- ¼ teaspoon black pepper
- ⅛ teaspoon salt

1. In a large nonstick skillet, cook zucchini, yellow squash, and onion in hot oil over medium heat for 8 to 10 minutes or until onion is just tender, stirring occasionally.
2. Add undrained green chiles, tomatoes, and dried oregano (if using). Heat through, stirring occasionally. Stir in fresh oregano (if using), black pepper, and salt. Serve immediately.
PER SERVING: 49 cal., 2 g total fat (0 g sat. fat), 0 mg chol., 112 mg sodium, 8 g carb., 2 g fiber, 2 g pro. Exchanges: 1.5 vegetable. Carb choices: 0.5.

Butternut Squash Kabobs
Think of this side as veggies on a stick. The kabobs are wonderful either hot or cold.
SERVINGS 8 (1 kabob each)
CARB. PER SERVING 7 g

- 1 2-pound butternut squash
- 3 tablespoon butter, melted
- 1 teaspoon curry powder
- ¼ teaspoon salt

1. Preheat oven to 450°F. Cut squash in half lengthwise and remove seeds. Peel squash. Cut squash halves into 1- to 1½-inch pieces. Place in a 3-quart rectangular baking dish. In a small bowl, combine butter and curry powder. Drizzle over squash, tossing to coat.
2. Roast squash, uncovered, for 20 to 25 minutes or until tender and lightly browned, stirring once or twice. Serve immediately or store in an airtight container in the refrigerator for up to 2 days.*
3. Serve squash at room temperature threaded on eight 8-inch skewers. Season with salt.
*TEST KITCHEN TIP: To reheat kabobs, grill on a charcoal grill directly over medium coals (or on a gas grill preheated to medium) about 10 minutes or until heated through, turning kabobs occasionally.
PER SERVING: 69 cal., 5 g total fat (2 g sat. fat), 12 mg chol., 36 mg sodium, 7 g carb., 1 g fiber, 1 g pro. Exchanges: 0.5 starch, 1 fat. Carb choices: 0.5.

Butternut Squash Kabobs

Squash, Corn, and Barley Succotash

The word "succotash" comes from a Native American word meaning boiled corn kernels. This version replaces the traditional lima beans with butternut squash.

SERVINGS 12 (about ½ cup each)
CARB. PER SERVING 23 g

 4 **cups water**
 ½ **cup regular barley**
 ¾ **teaspoon salt**
 1 **tablespoon olive oil**
 1 **cup finely chopped onion**
 1 **2-pound butternut squash, peeled, seeded, and cut into ½-inch cubes (about 4 cups)**
 ¾ **cup reduced-sodium chicken broth**
 ¼ **teaspoon black pepper**
 ⅛ **teaspoon dried thyme, crushed**
 3 **cups frozen whole kernel corn (about 12 ounces)**
 ¼ **cup chopped fresh parsley**

1. In a medium saucepan, bring water to boiling. Add barley and ½ teaspoon of the salt. Return to boiling; reduce heat. Cover and simmer about 40 minutes or until barley is tender, stirring occasionally. Drain and set aside.

2. Meanwhile, in a large skillet, heat oil over medium-high heat. Add onion; cook and stir about 5 minutes or until tender. Stir in the remaining ¼ teaspoon salt, the squash, broth, pepper, and thyme. Bring to boiling; reduce heat. Cover and simmer about 10 minutes or until squash is tender. Stir in corn; cover and cook for 5 minutes more. Stir in barley and parsley; heat through.

PER SERVING: 109 cal., 2 g total fat (0 g sat. fat), 0 mg chol., 187 mg sodium, 23 g carb., 4 g fiber, 3 g pro. Exchanges: 1.5 starch. Carb choices: 1.5.

Egglant-Zucchini
Parmesan

Eggplant-Zucchini Parmesan

*When your garden's bounty includes eggplant and
zucchini, this is the perfect recipe for you.*

SERVINGS 8 (¾ cup each)

CARB. PER SERVING 9 g

1 medium eggplant, peeled and cut into 1-inch cubes
1 medium zucchini, cut into 1-inch cubes
1 medium onion, cut into thin wedges
1½ cups light spaghetti sauce
⅓ cup shredded Parmesan cheese
   Shredded Parmesan cheese (optional)

1. In a 3½- or 4-quart slow cooker, combine eggplant, zucchini, onion, spaghetti sauce, and the ⅓ cup Parmesan cheese.

2. Cover and cook on low-heat setting for 4 to 5 hours or on high-heat setting for 2 to 2½ hours. If desired, sprinkle individual servings with additional Parmesan.

PER SERVING: 55 cal., 1 g total fat (1 g sat. fat), 2 mg chol., 210 mg sodium, 9 g carb., 3 g fiber, 3 g pro. Exchanges: 1 vegetable, 0.5 carb. Carb choices: 0.5.

Sweet Potato Fries

*For extra flavor, sprinkle on a little chili powder
and ground cumin before baking.*

SERVINGS 6 (scant 1 cup each)

CARB. PER SERVING 17 g

4 medium sweet potatoes, peeled if desired
2 tablespoons olive oil
¼ teaspoon salt
⅛ teaspoon black pepper
   Snipped fresh parsley (optional)

1. Preheat oven to 400°F. Line two baking sheets with foil.

2. Cut sweet potatoes lengthwise into ½-inch-thick strips. Place sweet potatoes in a large bowl. Drizzle with oil and toss to coat. Arrange sweet potatoes in a single layer on prepared baking sheets and bake for 10 to 15 minutes.

3. Turn potatoes over and bake for 10 to 15 minutes more or until golden brown. Sprinkle with salt and pepper. If desired, sprinkle with parsley.

PER SERVING: 114 cal., 5 g total fat (1 g sat. fat), 0 mg chol., 145 mg sodium, 17 g carb., 3 g fiber, 1 g pro. Exchanges: 1 starch, 1 fat. Carb choices: 1.

Sweet
Potato
Fries

eye-opening breakfasts

Rise to the occasion each day with a nutritious morning meal. Whether you choose an overnight egg casserole, a fast-fixin' breakfast burrito, a hearty whole grain cereal, or a fresh-from-the-oven muffin, set your day in motion with a great start.

Farmer's Casserole

This homey breakfast-style dish is delicious for supper, too. You can assemble it in the morning, chill it all day, and pop it into the oven just in time for a meal together.

SERVINGS 6 (1 piece each)
CARB. PER SERVING 23 g

    3   cups frozen shredded hashbrowns
    ¾   cup shredded Monterey Jack cheese with jalapeño
        peppers or shredded cheddar cheese (3 ounces)
    1   cup diced cooked ham or Canadian-style bacon
    ¼   cup sliced green onions
    1   cup refrigerated or frozen egg product, thawed, or
        4 eggs, lightly beaten
   1½   cups fat-free milk or one 12-ounce can evaporated
        fat-free milk
    ⅛   teaspoon black pepper

1. Preheat oven to 350°F. Coat a 2-quart square baking dish with *nonstick cooking spray.* Arrange potatoes evenly in the bottom of the dish. Sprinkle with cheese, ham, and green onions.
2. In a medium bowl, combine eggs, milk, and pepper. Pour egg mixture over potato mixture in dish.
3. Bake casserole, uncovered, for 40 to 45 minutes or until a knife inserted near the center comes out clean. Let stand for 5 minutes before serving. Cut into six pieces.
PER SERVING: 208 cal., 6 g total fat (3 g sat. fat), 27 mg chol., 610 mg sodium, 23 g carb., 2 g fiber, 17 g pro. Exchanges: 1.5 starch, 2 lean meat. Carb choices: 1.5.

Mexican-Style
Scrambled Eggs

> **QUICK TIP**
> For a pick-up-and-eat
> breakfast, fold in the
> sides of the tortilla
> and then roll it up to
> enclose the filling.

Mexican-Style Scrambled Eggs

*Extra-sharp cheddar cheese is more flavorful than
its milder cousins, so you don't have to use as much—
and that means fewer calories and less fat.*

SERVINGS 4 (1 filled tortilla each)

CARB. PER SERVING 20 g

 1   cup water
 ¼   cup thinly sliced green onions
 ¼   cup chopped red or green sweet pepper
 1   cup carton refrigerated or frozen egg product, thawed,
     or 4 eggs, lightly beaten
 ¼   cup fat-free milk
 ⅛   teaspoon black pepper
 4   7-inch whole wheat tortillas
 1   teaspoon butter
 ½   cup shredded reduced-fat cheddar cheese (2 ounces)
 ⅓   cup purchased fresh salsa
 ¼   cup light sour cream (optional)

1. Preheat oven to 350°F. In a small saucepan, combine
the water, green onions, and sweet pepper. Bring to
boiling; reduce heat. Simmer, uncovered, for 5 to
7 minutes or until vegetables are tender. Drain well.
In a medium bowl, stir together eggs, milk, and black
pepper. Stir in cooked vegetables.
2. Stack tortillas; wrap in foil. Bake about 10 minutes
or until warm. (Or just before serving, cover and
microwave tortillas on high [100% power] about
1 minute.)
3. Meanwhile, in a large skillet, melt butter over
medium heat. Pour in egg mixture. Cook, without
stirring, until mixture begins to set on bottom and
around edge. Using a spatula or large spoon, lift and fold
partially cooked eggs so uncooked portion flows
underneath. Sprinkle with cheese. Continue cooking for
2 to 3 minutes or until eggs are cooked through but still
glossy and moist.
4. To serve, immediately spoon egg mixture down the
center of each warm tortilla. Fold tortilla in half or roll
up. Top with salsa and, if desired, sour cream.
PER SERVING: 228 cal., 8 g total fat (4 g sat. fat), 13 mg chol.,
608 mg sodium, 20 g carb., 11 g fiber, 18 g pro. Exchanges:
1 starch, 2 lean meat, 1.5 fat. Carb choices: 1.

Cheese Quiche

Fat-free milk and low-fat cheeses transform ordinary quiche into a nutritious family pleaser.

SERVINGS 8 (1 wedge each)

CARB. PER SERVING 4 g

½ cup fat-free milk

2 tablespoons all-purpose flour

¾ cup refrigerated or frozen egg product, thawed, or 3 eggs, lightly beaten

1 cup low-fat cottage cheese

2 ounces reduced-fat cream cheese (Neufchâtel), cut up

1 cup shredded reduced-fat sharp cheddar cheese or Monterey Jack cheese (4 ounces)

⅛ teaspoon black pepper

Fresh chopped tomatoes (optional)

Chopped fresh basil or oregano (optional)

1. Preheat oven to 350°F. In a medium bowl, gradually whisk the milk into the flour until smooth. Whisk in the eggs, cottage cheese, and cream cheese (mixture will not be smooth). Stir in cheddar cheese and pepper.

2. Pour mixture into a lightly greased 9-inch pie plate. Bake for 45 to 50 minutes or until puffed and golden and a knife inserted near the center comes out clean. Cut into eight wedges. Serve immediately. If desired, garnish with tomatoes and fresh herbs.

PER SERVING: 107 cal., 5 g total fat (3 g sat. fat), 17 mg chol., 309 mg sodium, 4 g carb., 0 g fiber, 11 g pro. Exchanges: 2 lean meat, 0.5 fat. Carb choices: 0.

Cheese Quiche

Broccoli
Strata

Broccoli Strata

Like cow's milk, soymilk is a great source of protein. It is also cholesterol-free, contains cancer-fighting isoflavones, and is often fortified with calcium. Take your pick of milk to use in this make-ahead day starter.

SERVINGS 6 (1 piece each)
CARB. PER SERVING 21 g

- 2 cups fresh broccoli florets or 2 cups frozen broccoli cuts, thawed
- 4 cups 1-inch cubes country or crusty Italian bread
- 4 ounces process Swiss (or Gruyère) cheese, cut up
- 1½ cups refrigerated or frozen egg product, thawed, or 6 eggs, lightly beaten
- 1½ cups light plain soymilk or fat-free milk
- 1 tablespoon honey mustard
- ½ teaspoon salt
- ¼ teaspoon black pepper
- ¼ teaspoon ground nutmeg
- 4 green onions, thinly sliced

1. In a medium saucepan, cook broccoli, covered, in a small amount of boiling salted water for 3 minutes; drain. Rinse with cold running water until cool; drain.
2. In a greased 2-quart au gratin dish or baking dish, spread half of the bread cubes. Top with broccoli and cheese. Add remaining bread cubes.
3. In a bowl, combine eggs, milk, honey mustard, salt, pepper, and nutmeg. Pour egg mixture over mixture in baking dish. Sprinkle with onions. Cover; chill overnight.
4. Preheat oven to 325°F. Bake, uncovered, for 50 to 55 minutes or until an instant-read thermometer inserted in center registers 170°F. Let stand for 10 minutes before serving. Cut into six pieces.
PER SERVING: 210 cal., 7 g total fat (4 g sat. fat), 17 mg chol., 581 mg sodium, 21 g carb., 2 g fiber, 15 g pro. Exchanges: 0.5 vegetable, 1 starch, 2 lean meat, 0.5 fat. Carb choices: 1.5.

Tomato-Broccoli Frittata

If you like, replace the feta cheese with goat, Parmesan, or fontina cheese.

SERVINGS 4 (1 wedge each)
CARB. PER SERVING 7 g

- 6 egg whites
- 3 eggs
- ¼ teaspoon salt
- ¼ teaspoon black pepper
- ¼ cup crumbled reduced-fat feta cheese or regular feta cheese
- 2 cups small broccoli florets
- 2 tablespoons finely chopped shallots
- 1 teaspoon olive oil
- 1¼ cups cherry tomatoes, quartered

1. Preheat broiler. In a bowl, whisk together egg whites, eggs, salt, and pepper. Stir in cheese; set aside.
2. In a large broilerproof skillet, cook broccoli and shallots in hot oil over medium heat for 8 to 10 minutes or just until tender, stirring occasionally. Pour egg mixture over the broccoli mixture in skillet. Cook over medium-low heat. As mixture sets, run a spatula around the edge of the skillet, lifting egg mixture so uncooked portion flows underneath. Continue cooking and lifting edge until egg mixture is almost set (surface will be moist). Arrange tomatoes on top of egg mixture.
3. Broil 4 to 5 inches from the heat about 5 minutes or until center is set. Let stand for 5 minutes before serving. Cut into four wedges.
PER SERVING: 134 cal., 6 g total fat (2 g sat. fat), 161 mg chol., 416 mg sodium, 7 g carb., 2 g fiber, 14 g pro. Exchanges: 1 vegetable, 2 lean meat. Carb choices: 0.5.

Tomato-Broccoli Frittata

Salmon Eggs Benedict

For classic Benedict, use Canadian-style bacon.

SERVINGS 4 (1 topped bread slice each)

CARB. PER SERVING 20 g

- ¼ cup light sour cream
- 1 teaspoon lemon juice
- ¾ to 1 teaspoon dry mustard
- 3 to 4 teaspoons fat-free milk
- 4 eggs
- 4 ½-inch-thick slices crusty French bread or French bread, lightly toasted
- ¼ pound thinly sliced smoked salmon or 4 slices Canadian-style bacon
  Diced red sweet pepper (optional)
  Black pepper

1. In a bowl, combine sour cream, lemon juice, and dry mustard. Add milk to desired consistency. Set aside.

2. Lightly grease 4 cups of an egg poaching pan.* Place the poacher cups over boiling water (water should not touch bottoms of cups); reduce heat to simmering. Break an egg into a measuring cup. Carefully slide egg into poacher cup. Repeat with remaining eggs. Cover; cook 6 to 8 minutes or until the whites are completely

Salmon Eggs Benedict

set and yolks begin to thicken but are not hard. Run a knife around edges to loosen eggs. Invert poacher cups to remove eggs.

3. Top each bread slice with smoked salmon. Top with a poached egg. Top with mustard-sour cream mixture and red sweet pepper. Season to taste with pepper.

*TEST KITCHEN TIP: If you don't have an egg-poaching pan, lightly grease a 2-quart saucepan with cooking oil or shortening. Fill the pan halfway with water; bring to boiling. Reduce heat to simmering. Break one egg into a measuring cup. Carefully slide egg into water, holding the lip of the cup as close to the water as possible. Repeat with remaining eggs, spacing eggs equally. Simmer, uncovered, for 3 to 5 minutes or until whites are completely set and yolks begin to thicken but are not hard. Remove eggs with a slotted spoon.

PER SERVING: 217 cal., 8 g total fat (3 g sat. fat), 222 mg chol., 510 mg sodium, 20 g carb., 1 g fiber, 16 g pro. Exchanges: 1 starch, 2 medium-fat meat. Carb choices: 1.

Cheesy Mushroom Casserole

A Southern breakfast favorite, hominy grits forms the base for this hearty egg casserole. Team it with a fresh fruit compote and bran muffins for a terrific company brunch.

SERVINGS 6 (1⅓ cups each)

CARB. PER SERVING 23 g

- 1 cup quick-cooking (hominy) grits
- ¾ cup shredded reduced-fat cheddar cheese (3 ounces)
- ⅛ teaspoon salt
- 1 8-ounce package sliced fresh button mushrooms
- 1 6-ounce package sliced fresh portobello mushrooms or two 3-ounce portobello mushrooms, cleaned and sliced
- ¼ teaspoon black pepper
- 4 ounces thinly sliced prosciutto, chopped
- 2 cloves garlic, minced
- 4 egg whites, lightly beaten
- 2 eggs, lightly beaten
  Snipped fresh parsley (optional)

1. Preheat oven to 350°F. Coat a 2-quart rectangular baking dish with *nonstick cooking spray*; set aside. In a large saucepan, bring 3 cups *water* to boiling. Gradually stir in grits. Reduce heat to low. Cook, uncovered, for 5 to 7 minutes or until thick, stirring frequently. Remove from heat. Stir in ¼ cup of the cheese and the salt. Spread evenly in the prepared dish.

2. Coat an unheated large nonstick skillet with *nonstick cooking spray*. Preheat skillet over medium heat. Add mushrooms and pepper. Cook about 5 minutes or until tender and any liquid is evaporated, stirring occasionally. Add prosciutto and garlic. Cook and stir for 1 minute more. Cool slightly.

3. Add egg whites and eggs to the mushroom mixture; stir to combine. Spread over grits in dish. Sprinkle with the remaining ½ cup cheese. Bake, uncovered, for 25 to 30 minutes or until heated through and egg mixture is set in center. Let stand for 5 minutes before serving. If desired, sprinkle with parsley.

PER SERVING: 235 cal., 10 g total fat (2 g sat. fat), 81 mg chol., 571 mg sodium, 23 g carb., 2 g fiber, 17 g pro. Exchanges: 0.5 vegetable, 1.5 starch, 1.5 medium-fat meat. Carb choices: 1.5.

Pineapple-Glazed Banana
Blueberry Muffins

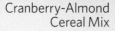

Cranberry-Almond
Cereal Mix
recipe on page 120

Kick-Start Activity

Being active, even if your abilities have become limited, is as important in diabetes control as your eating habits. Use these tips to work exercise into your daily regime.

1. **Reflect on resistance.** Think about what has caused your shift in exercise drive.

2. **Validate your feelings.** Adopt kindness for yourself instead of criticism. Self-understanding opens up a willingness to consider activity on your own terms.

3. **Pick a start day.** Decide when you will begin to exercise. On that date, celebrate the activity.

4. **Explore activities you enjoy.** Yoga, line dancing, tennis? Choose any activity that revs your engine, even if you have to adapt moves for a seated position.

5. **Put it in writing.** Create a document that states why, when, and how you will exercise.

6. **Set a time.** Just get started, no excuses.

Lemon Poppy Seed
Muffins

Pineapple-Glazed Banana Blueberry Muffins

The bananas lend extra moisture to the muffins, while the glaze of pineapple preserves adds a sweet note.

SERVINGS 12 (1 muffin each)

CARB. PER SERVING 31 g or 25 g

1¾ cups all-purpose flour
⅓ cup packed brown sugar*
2 teaspoons baking powder
½ teaspoon ground cinnamon
¼ teaspoon salt
¾ cup mashed ripe banana
½ cup fat-free milk
¼ cup butter, melted
¼ cup refrigerated or frozen egg product, thawed, or
  1 egg, lightly beaten
1 teaspoon vanilla
¾ cup fresh blueberries
¼ cup pineapple preserves

1. Preheat oven to 400°F. Grease twelve 2½-inch muffin cups; set aside.
2. In a medium bowl, stir together flour, brown sugar, baking powder, cinnamon, and salt. Make a well in center of flour mixture; set aside.
3. In a another medium bowl, combine banana, milk, melted butter, egg, and vanilla. Add banana mixture all at once to flour mixture. Stir just until moistened (batter will be lumpy). Fold in blueberries. Spoon batter into prepared muffin cups, filling each three-fourths full. Spoon 1 teaspoon pineapple preserves onto batter in each muffin cup.
4. Bake for 15 to 20 minutes or until golden and a wooden toothpick inserted in centers comes out clean. Cool in muffin cups on a wire rack for 5 minutes. Remove from muffin cups. Serve warm.

***SUGAR SUBSTITUTES:** Choose from Sweet'N Low Brown or Sugar Twin Granulated Brown. Follow package directions to use product amount equivalent to ⅓ cup brown sugar.
PER SERVING: 172 cal., 4 g total fat (3 g sat. fat), 11 mg chol., 135 mg sodium, 31 g carb., 2 g fiber, 3 g pro. Exchanges: 2 carb., 0.5 fat. Carb choices: 2.
PER SERVING WITH SUBSTITUTE: Same as above, except 150 cal., 132 mg sodium, 25 g carb. Exchanges: 1.5 carb., 0.5 fat Carb. choices: 1.5.

Lemon Poppy Seed Muffins

Bakers have used poppy seeds to decorate breads and cakes since the days of ancient Egypt and Rome. Here, the seeds add both texture and flavor.

SERVINGS 12 (1 muffin each)

CARB. PER SERVING 24 g or 20 g

1¾ cups all-purpose flour
½ cup granulated sugar*
1 tablespoon poppy seeds
1 tablespoon finely shredded lemon peel
2 teaspoons baking powder
½ teaspoon salt
¾ cup fat-free milk
¼ cup refrigerated or frozen egg product, thawed, or
  1 egg, lightly beaten
¼ cup canola oil
2 teaspoons coarse sugar

1. Preheat oven to 375°F. Lightly coat twelve 2½-inch muffin cups with *nonstick cooking spray* or line with paper bake cups (spray insides of paper bake cups with nonstick cooking spray). Set muffin cups aside.
2. In a medium bowl, stir together flour, granulated sugar, poppy seeds, lemon peel, baking powder, and salt. Make a well in center of flour mixture; set aside.
3. In another medium bowl, combine milk, egg, and oil. Add egg mixture all at once to flour mixture. Stir just until moistened (batter will be lumpy). Spoon batter into prepared muffin cups, filling each two-thirds full. Sprinkle tops with coarse sugar.
4. Bake for 20 to 25 minutes or until golden and a wooden toothpick inserted in centers comes out clean. Cool in muffin cups on a wire rack for 5 minutes. Remove from muffin cups. Serve warm.

***SUGAR SUBSTITUTES:** Choose Splenda Sugar Blend for Baking. Follow package directions to use product amount equivalent to ½ cup sugar.
PER SERVING: 150 cal., 5 g total fat (0 g sat. fat), 0 mg chol., 153 mg sodium, 24 g carb., 1 g fiber, 3 g pro. Exchanges: 1.5 carb., 0.5 fat. Carb choices: 1.5.
PER SERVING WITH SUBSTITUTE: Same as above, except 137 cal., 20 g carb. Exchanges: 1 carb. Carb. choices: 1.

Pear-Cheddar
Quick Bread

2. Combine pears, eggs, sugar, oil, buttermilk, honey, and vanilla; add all at once to flour mixture. Stir until combined. Fold in cheese. Spoon batter into pan.

3. Bake for 50 to 55 minutes (45 to 50 minutes for the smaller pans) or until a wooden toothpick inserted near center comes out clean. Cool in pan on a wire rack for 10 minutes. Remove from pan. Cool on a wire rack.

*SUGAR SUBSTITUTES: We do not recommend sugar substitutes for this recipe.

PER SERVING: 164 cal., 6 g total fat (1 g sat. fat), 4 mg chol., 107 mg sodium, 24 g carb., 2 g fiber, 4 g pro. Exchanges: 1.5 carb., 1 fat. Carb choices: 1.5.

Breakfast Fruit-and-Nut Cookies

Wrap cookies individually and stash in the freezer. Then on a morning when you're racing out the door, grab one of these fully loaded breakfast treats.

SERVINGS 10 (1 cookie each)

CARB. PER SERVING 35 g

½ cup refrigerated or frozen egg product, thawed, or 2 eggs, lightly beaten
⅔ cup packed brown sugar
3 tablespoons butter, melted
1 teaspoon vanilla
¼ cup finely snipped dried fruit (dates, apricots, or figs)
1 cup all-purpose flour
½ cup whole wheat flour
¼ cup oat bran
2 tablespoons ground flaxseeds
½ teaspoon baking soda
½ teaspoon ground cinnamon
¼ cup chopped pecans or walnuts, toasted

1. Preheat oven to 350°F. Line two cookie sheets with parchment paper; set aside. In a bowl, combine eggs, brown sugar, butter, and vanilla. Stir in dates; set aside.

2. In a medium bowl, combine all-purpose flour, whole wheat flour, oat bran, flaxseeds, baking soda, and cinnamon. Add flour mixture to date mixture; stir until moist. Stir in pecans.

3. Using a scant ¼ cup measure, drop dough into 10 mounds about 2 inches apart onto prepared cookie sheets and lightly flatten cookies. Bake for 10 to 12 minutes or until edges are golden. Cool on cookie sheets for 1 minute. Transfer to a wire rack; cool.

PER SERVING: 207 cal., 6 g total fat (2 g sat. fat), 9 mg chol., 116 mg sodium, 35 g carb., 3 g fiber, 5 g pro. Exchanges: 2 carb., 1 fat. Carb choices: 2.

Pear-Cheddar Quick Bread

For superb flavor and easier slicing, wrap the cooled loaf and store it overnight in the refrigerator. Then let it stand at room temperature for 1 hour before slicing.

SERVINGS 16 (1 slice each)

CARB. PER SERVING 24 g

1⅓ cups all-purpose flour
½ cup whole wheat pastry flour or whole wheat flour
¼ cup flaxseed meal or toasted wheat germ
2 teaspoons baking powder
1½ cups shredded cored unpeeled pears (about 1½ medium pears)
½ cup refrigerated or frozen egg product, thawed, or 2 eggs, lightly beaten
½ cup sugar*
⅓ cup canola oil
¼ cup buttermilk or sour milk
¼ cup honey
1 teaspoon vanilla
½ cup shredded white cheddar cheese (2 ounces)

1. Preheat oven to 350°F. Grease the bottom and ½ inch up the sides of one 9×5×3-inch loaf pan or two 7×3½×2-inch loaf pans; set aside. In a large bowl, combine flours, flaxseed meal, baking powder, and ¼ teaspoon *salt*. Make a well in center of the flour mixture; set aside.

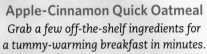

Apple-Cinnamon Quick Oatmeal
*Grab a few off-the-shelf ingredients for
a tummy-warming breakfast in minutes.*

SERVINGS 4 (about ¾ cup each)
CARB. PER SERVING 32 g

1½ cups water
¾ cup apple juice
½ cup chopped dried apples
1¼ cups quick-cooking rolled oats
1 teaspoon ground cinnamon
½ cup plain fat-free yogurt

1. In a medium saucepan, combine water, apple juice, and dried apples. Bring to boiling. In a small bowl, combine oats and cinnamon; add to boiling water mixture. Cook for 1 minute, stirring occasionally.
2. Divide hot oatmeal among four bowls. Top each serving with a spoonful of yogurt.

PER SERVING: 162 cal., 2 g total fat (0 g sat. fat), 1 mg chol., 39 mg sodium, 32 g carb., 4 g fiber, 5 g pro. Exchanges: 1 fruit, 1 starch. Carb choices: 2.

Honey-Ginger Compote

Cranberry-Almond Cereal Mix

Keep this cereal mixture on hand and cook one or two servings at a time. Pictured on page 116.

SERVINGS 14 (⅓ cup dry mix each)
CARB. PER SERVING 33 g or 29 g

  1 cup regular rolled oats
  1 cup quick-cooking barley
  1 cup bulgur, cracked wheat, or amaranth seeds
  ¾ cup dried cranberries, snipped dried apricots, or raisins
  ¾ cup sliced almonds, toasted
  ¼ cup sugar*
  1 tablespoon ground cinnamon
  ¼ teaspoon salt
     Fat-free milk (optional)

1. In a large bowl, stir together oats, barley, bulgur, cranberries, almonds, sugar, cinnamon, and salt. Cover tightly and store at room temperature for up to 2 months or freeze for up to 6 months (stir or shake mixture before measuring).

2. For 2 servings: In a small saucepan, bring 1⅓ cups *water* to boiling. Add ⅔ cup of the cereal mix. Reduce heat. Simmer, covered, for 14 to 16 minutes or until grains are tender and cereal reaches desired consistency, stirring occasionally. If desired, serve with milk.

MICROWAVE DIRECTIONS: For 1 serving: In a 1-quart microwave-safe bowl, combine ¾ cup water and ⅓ cup cereal mix. Microwave, covered, on medium (50% power) for 10 to 12 minutes or until grains are tender and cereal reaches desired consistency, stirring once. Stir before serving. If desired, serve with milk.

*SUGAR SUBSTITUTES: Choose from Splenda granular or Sweet'N Low bulk or packets. Follow package directions to use product amount equivalent to ¼ cup sugar.

PER SERVING: 166 cal., 3 g total fat (0 g sat. fat), 0 mg chol., 44 mg sodium, 33 g carb., 5 g fiber, 4 g pro. Exchanges: 0.5 fruit, 1.5 starch. Carb choices: 2.

PER SERVING WITH SUBSTITUTE: Same as above, except 154 cal., 29 g carb.

Honey-Ginger Compote

Imagine the good impression this spicy fruit compote will make when you bring it to the table in stemmed glasses! Add a sprig of mint to each serving for a cool summertime accent.

SERVINGS 2 (¾ cup each)
CARB. PER SERVING 27 g

  ¼ cup apple juice, apple cider, or unsweetened pineapple juice
  2 teaspoons honey
  1 teaspoon finely chopped crystallized ginger
  1 teaspoon lemon juice
  1½ cups assorted fruit (such as cubed melon, sliced star fruit [carambola], halved grapes, raspberries, pitted sweet cherries, cubed peaches, cubed pears, cubed mango, sliced kiwifruit, and/or chopped pineapple)
  2 tablespoons low-fat vanilla yogurt with artificial sweetener (optional)

1. In a small saucepan, combine apple juice, honey, crystallized ginger, and lemon juice. Cook and stir over medium heat until boiling. Transfer to a small bowl; cover and refrigerate for 4 to 48 hours.

2. To serve, toss together assorted fruit. Spoon into tall stemmed glasses or dessert dishes. Pour apple juice mixture over fruit. If desired, spoon yogurt on top of fruit mixture.

PER SERVING: 103 cal., 0 g total fat, 0 mg chol., 10 mg sodium, 27 g carb., 1 g fiber, 1 g pro. Exchanges: 1 fruit, 0.5 carb.. Carb choices: 2.

QUICK TIP ◖
Add a little frost to the glasses by placing them in the freezer about 30 minutes before whirling together these smoothies.

Fresh Figs with Yogurt and Honey

Summer through early fall is the prime time to find fresh figs at the supermarket.

SERVINGS 2 (about ⅔ cup each)

CARB. PER SERVING 22 g

- 1 6-ounce carton plain low-fat yogurt
- ½ teaspoon vanilla
- 2 fresh figs or apricots, cut up
- 1 tablespoon coarsely chopped walnuts, toasted
- 2 teaspoons honey
- Finely shredded lemon peel (optional)

1. Set a strainer lined with 100%-cotton cheesecloth or a paper coffee filter over a large mug. Spoon yogurt into lined strainer. Cover and chill for at least 8 hours or up to 24 hours. (Yogurt will thicken to form a soft cheese.)
2. Discard liquid in mug. In a small bowl, gently stir together the thickened yogurt and vanilla; fold in figs or apricots. Spoon into two small dessert dishes. Sprinkle with walnuts. Drizzle individual servings with honey. If desired, sprinkle with lemon peel.
PER SERVING: 139 cal., 4 g total fat (1 g sat. fat), 5 mg chol., 60 mg sodium, 22 g carb., 2 g fiber, 5 g pro. Exchanges: 0.5 milk, 1 fruit, 0.5 fat. Carb choices: 1.5.

Strawberry-Pineapple Smoothies

Sliced banana is a delicious substitute for the mango.

SERVINGS 6 (6 ounces each)

CARB. PER SERVING 12 g

- 2 cups fresh strawberries, halved and chilled
- 1 cup chopped fresh pineapple
- ¾ cup chopped bottled or fresh mango
- ⅓ cup unsweetened pineapple juice
- 2 cups ice cubes
- Fresh strawberries or pineapple chunks (optional)

1. In a blender, combine strawberries, pineapple, mango, and pineapple juice. Cover and blend until smooth. With blender running, gradually add ice cubes through opening in lid. Blend until smooth after each addition. Serve immediately in chilled glasses. If desired, garnish individual servings with strawberries.
PER SERVING: 48 cal., 0 g total fat, 0 mg chol., 1 mg sodium, 12 g carb., 2 g fiber, 1 g pro. Exchanges: 1 fruit. Carb choices: 1.

Strawberry-Pineapple Smoothies

good-for-you
snacks

A few nibbles of a nutritious snack between hearty main meals can keep your blood glucose levels in check throughout the day. Stir together one of these diabetes-friendly recipes to munch on when you need a little something to help you feel good all day long.

Pepper Cheese with Apricots

Hot and sweet flavors—black pepper and apricots—comingle perfectly in this creamy yogurt cheese spread.

SERVINGS 12 (2 tablespoons dip and 4 crackers each)
CARB. PER SERVING 17 g

1   16-ounce carton plain low-fat yogurt*
¼   cup finely snipped dried apricots
1   tablespoon honey
¼   to ½ teaspoon coarsely ground black pepper
½   of an 8-ounce package reduced-fat cream cheese (Neufchâtel), softened (½ cup)
1   tablespoon finely chopped pistachio nuts
48   low-fat whole grain crackers

1. Line a large strainer or yogurt sieve with a double thickness of 100%-cotton cheesecloth. Place strainer or sieve over a medium bowl. Stir together yogurt, apricots, honey, and pepper. Spoon mixture into strainer. Cover and refrigerate for 4 to 24 hours or until mixture is firm.

2. Discard any liquid in bowl; wash and dry bowl. Transfer yogurt mixture to clean bowl; stir in cream cheese. Sprinkle with nuts. Serve with crackers.

*TEST KITCHEN TIP: Use a brand of yogurt that contains no gums, gelatin, or fillers. These ingredients may prevent the whey from separating from the curd to make cheese.

PER SERVING: 123 cal., 5 g total fat (2 g sat. fat), 9 mg chol., 138 mg sodium, 17 g carb., 2 g fiber, 5 g pro. Exchanges: 1 starch, 1 fat. Carb choices: 1.

Kickoff Pepper Dip

A sweet pepper puree, horseradish, and bottled hot pepper sauce blend with cream cheese and mayonnaise for a dynamite dip for veggies.

SERVINGS 10 (¼ cup dip and ¾ cup vegetable dippers each)

CARB. PER SERVING 11 g

- 4 large red, green, yellow, or orange sweet peppers, cut up
- 1 small onion, cut up
- ¼ cup water
- 1 8-ounce package reduced-fat cream cheese (Neufchâtel), softened
- ¼ cup low-fat mayonnaise dressing or light salad dressing
- 2 tablespoons lemon juice
- 2 teaspoons olive oil or cooking oil
- 1 teaspoon prepared horseradish
- ¼ teaspoon salt
  Few dashes bottled hot pepper sauce
  Freshly ground black pepper (optional)
- 7½ cups assorted vegetable dippers (such as carrot sticks, sweet pepper strips, sliced zucchini, and/or celery sticks)

1. In a blender or large food processor, combine one-third of the cut-up sweet peppers, the onion, and the water. Blend or process until smooth. Add the remaining cut-up peppers; cover and blend until smooth.

2. Place pureed vegetable mixture in a fine sieve; press mixture gently to drain off excess liquid. Set aside.

3. In a bowl, combine cream cheese, mayonnaise dressing, lemon juice, oil, horseradish, salt, and hot pepper sauce. Beat with an electric mixer on medium speed. Beat in pureed vegetable mixture. Cover and chill for at least 4 hours or up to 12 hours. If desired, sprinkle dip with black pepper. Serve with vegetable dippers.

PER SERVING: 116 cal., 7 g total fat (4 g sat. fat), 17 mg chol., 239 mg sodium, 11 g carb., 3 g fiber, 4 g pro. Exchanges: 1.5 vegetable, 1.5 fat. Carb choices: 1.

Carrot Hummus

Carrots add more than color and sweetness to this spicy hummus. Their abundance of beta-carotene, combined with the health attributes of garbanzo beans, makes this dip a healthful choice.

SERVINGS 16 (2 tablespoons hummus and 4 pita wedges each)

CARB. PER SERVING 25 g

- 1 cup chopped carrots
- 1 15-ounce can garbanzo beans (chickpeas), rinsed and drained
- ¼ cup tahini (sesame seed paste)
- 2 tablespoons lemon juice
- 2 cloves garlic, quartered
- ½ teaspoon ground cumin
- 2 tablespoons snipped fresh parsley
- 8 whole wheat pita bread rounds, cut into 8 wedges each and toasted, or 8 cups vegetable sticks

1. In a covered small saucepan, cook carrots in a small amount of boiling water for 6 to 8 minutes or until tender; drain. In a food processor, combine cooked carrots, the garbanzo beans, tahini, lemon juice, garlic, cumin, and ¼ teaspoon *salt*. Process until mixture is smooth. Transfer mixture to a bowl. Stir in parsley. Cover and chill for at least 1 hour or up to 3 days. If too thick, stir in water, 1 tablespoon at a time, until dipping consistency. Serve with pitas or vegetables.

PER SERVING: 144 cal., 3 g total fat (0 g sat. fat), 0 mg chol., 287 mg sodium, 25 g carb., 4 g fiber, 5 g pro. Exchanges: 1.5 starch, 0.5 fat. Carb choices: 1.5.

Kickoff
Pepper Dip

Mediterranean
Veggie Dip

Mediterranean Veggie Dip

If your meal plan allows, serve this tangy herb dip with crackerlike flatbread. If not, stick to crunchy fresh vegetables.

SERVINGS 12 (2 tablespoons dip and ½ cup vegetables each)

CARB. PER SERVING 7 g

- 1 recipe Yogurt Cheese (right)
- ¼ cup chopped roasted red sweet peppers
- ¼ cup crumbled reduced-fat feta cheese
- 2 tablespoons thinly sliced green onion
- 2 tablespoons chopped pitted kalamata or black olives
- 2 tablespoons snipped fresh flat-leaf (Italian) parsley
- 2 teaspoons snipped fresh oregano or ½ teaspoon dried oregano, crushed
- 6 cups carrot sticks, broccoli florets, cucumber spears, and/or sweet pepper strips

1. In a small bowl, combine Yogurt Cheese, roasted sweet peppers, feta cheese, green onion, olives, parsley, and oregano. Cover and chill for up to 24 hours. Stir before serving. Serve with vegetables.

YOGURT CHEESE: Line a yogurt strainer, sieve, or a small colander with a double thickness of 100%-cotton cheesecloth or a clean paper coffee filter. Suspend lined strainer, sieve, or colander over a bowl. Spoon in one 16-ounce carton plain low-fat yogurt.* Cover with plastic wrap. Chill for at least 24 hours. Drain and discard liquid. Store, covered, in refrigerator for up to 1 week.

***TEST KITCHEN TIP:** Use a brand of yogurt that contains no gums, gelatin, or fillers. These ingredients may prevent the whey from separating from the curd to make cheese.

PER SERVING: 50 cal., 1 g total fat (1 g sat. fat), 3 mg chol., 103 mg sodium, 7 g carb., 1 g fiber, 3 g pro. Exchanges: 0.5 milk, 0.5 vegetable. Carb choices: 0.5.

▶ QUICK TIP

Turn leftover hummus into a totable lunch. Spread it on a whole grain wrap and top with cucumber, roasted sweet peppers, and fresh spinach. Roll up.

Hummus and Cucumber Bruschetta

Black-Eyed Peas Salsa

Grab a can of black beans or small white kidney beans as a protein alternative to the black-eyed peas.

SERVINGS 8 (¼ cup dip and ½ ounce chips each)
CARB. PER SERVING 22 g

1   15-ounce can black-eyed peas, rinsed and drained
¼   cup thinly sliced green onions
¼   cup finely chopped red sweet pepper
2   tablespoons canola oil
2   tablespoons cider vinegar
1   to 2 fresh jalapeño chile peppers, seeded and chopped (see tip, page 96)
¼   teaspoon cracked black pepper
    Dash salt
2   cloves garlic, minced
4   ounces baked tortilla chips

1. In a medium bowl, combine black-eyed peas, green onions, sweet pepper, oil, vinegar, jalapeño pepper, black pepper, salt, and garlic. Cover and chill overnight. Serve with tortilla chips.
PER SERVING: 142 cal., 4 g total fat (0 g sat. fat), 0 mg chol., 271 mg sodium, 22 g carb., 4 g fiber, 5 g pro. Exchanges: 1.5 starch, 0.5 fat. Carb choices: 1.5.

Hummus and Cucumber Bruschetta

If you wish, pick up a whole wheat baguette-style loaf to make these crispy toasts.

SERVINGS 4 (3 topped bread slices each)
CARB. PER SERVING 21 g

12   ¼-inch slices baguette-style French bread
     Olive oil nonstick cooking spray
1½   teaspoons Italian seasoning, crushed
¼   teaspoon garlic powder
⅓   cup finely chopped English cucumber
2   tablespoons plain low-fat yogurt
1½   teaspoons lemon juice
1½   teaspoons snipped fresh oregano or ½ teaspoon dried oregano, crushed
⅓   cup hummus
¼   cup chopped roasted red sweet peppers
     Snipped fresh oregano (optional)

1. Preheat oven to 400°F. Arrange baguette slices in a single layer on a large baking sheet. Lightly coat baguette slices with cooking spray. Combine Italian seasoning and garlic powder; sprinkle over bread. Bake 10 minutes or until slices are crisp and lightly browned.

2. Meanwhile, in a small bowl, combine cucumber, yogurt, lemon juice, and the 1½ teaspoons fresh or ½ teaspoon dried oregano. Spread some of the hummus on top of each toasted baguette slice; top with cucumber mixture and roasted red peppers. If desired, sprinkle with additional fresh oregano.

FRUIT BRUSCHETTA: Prepare as directed, except lightly coat baguette slices with regular nonstick cooking spray. Omit Italian seasoning and garlic powder. Bake as directed; cool. Substitute finely chopped mango and/or blood oranges or oranges for cucumber and light cream cheese spread with strawberries for the hummus. Omit lemon juice. Substitute snipped fresh mint for oregano.

PER SERVING: 126 cal., 3 g total fat (0 g sat. fat), 0 mg chol., 296 mg sodium, 21 g carb., 1 g fiber, 5 g pro. Exchanges: 1.5 starch. Carb choices: 1.5.

Spicy Tofu Lettuce Wraps

Antipasto Kabobs

The variety of textures, colors, and flavors in this recipe makes it the perfect prelude to virtually any entrée. These no-cook kabobs can also make satisfying snacks.

SERVINGS 6 (2 kabobs each)

CARB. PER SERVING 3 g

1½ to 2 cups assorted fresh vegetables (such as baby carrots, halved radishes, sweet pepper squares, whole miniature sweet peppers, and/or halved pattypan squash)

2 ounces part-skim mozzarella cheese, provolone cheese, or smoked Gouda cheese, cut into ½-inch pieces

2 ounces cooked smoked turkey sausage, cut into ¾-inch-thick slices and quartered

2 tablespoons refrigerated basil pesto

1 tablespoon white wine vinegar

12 whole fresh basil leaves

1. Place vegetables, cheese, and sausage in a resealable plastic bag set in a shallow bowl. For marinade: In a small bowl, stir together pesto and vinegar; pour over vegetable mixture. Seal bag; turn to coat vegetable mixture. Marinate in the refrigerator for 1 to 24 hours, turning bag occasionally.

2. On twelve 4-inch-long wooden skewers, alternately thread vegetables, cheese, sausage, and basil leaves.

PER SERVING: 84 cal., 6 g total fat (2 g sat. fat), 13 mg chol., 188 mg sodium, 3 g carb., 1 g fiber, 5 g pro. Exchanges: 0.5 vegetable, 0.5 lean meat, 1 fat. Carb choices: 0.

Spicy Tofu Lettuce Wraps

For easier chopping, cut the cube of tofu into large pieces before adding to the food processor.

SERVINGS 8 (1 wrap each)

CARB. PER SERVING 12 g

12 ounces extra-firm tofu (fresh bean curd)

2 cups shredded cabbage with carrot (coleslaw mix)

1 8-ounce can sliced water chestnuts, drained

2 green onions, chopped

2 tablespoons snipped fresh cilantro

⅓ cup Asian sweet chili sauce or bottled stir-fry sauce

1 tablespoon lime juice

8 large leaves butterhead (Boston or Bibb) lettuce or green leaf lettuce

1. Drain tofu; press out excess liquid with paper towels. In a food processor, combine about half the tofu, coleslaw mix, water chestnuts, green onions, and cilantro. Cover and process with several on/off pulses until finely chopped. Transfer to a large skillet. Repeat with the remaining tofu, coleslaw mix, water chestnuts, green onions, and cilantro. Stir chili sauce and lime juice into mixture in skillet. Cook and stir over medium heat until heated.

2. Cut the center veins, if present, from lettuce leaves. Divide tofu mixture among lettuce leaves; fold or roll up. Secure with picks.

PER SERVING: 88 cal., 2 g total fat (0 g sat. fat), 0 mg chol., 141 mg sodium, 12 g carb., 3 g fiber, 5 g pro. Exchanges: 1 vegetable, 0.5 carb., 0.5 medium-fat meat. Carb choices: 1.

Peanut Butter
Cereal Bars

Sugar 'n' Spice
Fruit Dip

Sugar 'n' Spice Fruit Dip

Choose your flavor—any low-sugar fruit preserves will work in this creamy concoction.

SERVINGS 10 (2 tablespoons dip and ½ cup fruit dippers each)

CARB. PER SERVING 14 g

½ cup tub-style light cream cheese, softened
½ cup light sour cream
¼ cup low-sugar raspberry preserves or orange marmalade
1 teaspoon finely shredded lemon peel or orange peel (optional)
¼ teaspoon ground cinnamon, nutmeg, or allspice
5 cups desired fruit dippers (such as clementine orange segments; strawberries; cut-up, peeled kiwifruit; raspberries; apple slices; pear slices; and/or banana slices)

1. In a medium bowl, beat cream cheese and sour cream with an electric mixer on medium speed until smooth. Stir in preserves, lemon peel (if desired), and cinnamon until well combined. If desired, sprinkle with additional *cinnamon.* Serve with fruit dippers.

TEST KITCHEN TIP: If desired, substitute 1 recipe Yogurt Cheese (page 125) for the sour cream and cream cheese.

PER SERVING: 89 cal., 3 g total fat (2 g sat. fat), 9 mg chol., 68 mg sodium, 14 g carb., 2 g fiber, 2 g pro. Exchanges: 1 fruit, 0.5 fat. Carb choices: 1.

Peanut Butter Cereal Bars

Two kinds of cereal, dried apples, honey, and chunky peanut butter make these snack bars delectable.

SERVINGS 16 (1 bar each)

CARB. PER SERVING 26 g

4 cups sweetened oat cereal flakes with raisins
¾ cup quick-cooking rolled oats
½ cup all-purpose flour
½ cup snipped dried apples
2 eggs
⅓ cup honey
⅓ cup chunky peanut butter
¼ cup canola oil or butter, melted

1. Preheat oven to 325°F. Line a 9×9×2-inch baking pan with foil. Coat foil with *nonstick cooking spray;* set aside. In a large bowl, combine oat cereal flakes, rolled oats, flour, and dried apples. Set aside.

2. In a small bowl, beat eggs with a fork; stir in honey, peanut butter, and oil. Pour over cereal mixture. Mix well. Transfer mixture to prepared pan. Using the back of a large spoon, press mixture firmly into pan. Bake for 28 to 30 minutes or until edges are browned. Cool in pan on a wire rack. Using a serrated knife, cut into bars.

TEST KITCHEN TIP: To store, wrap bars individually in plastic wrap. Store in the refrigerator for up to 3 days. For longer storage, place individually wrapped bars in a freezer container or freezer bag; freeze for up to 3 months. To serve, thaw in refrigerator overnight.

PER SERVING: 181 cal., 8 g total fat (1 g sat. fat), 27 mg chol., 91 mg sodium, 26 g carb., 2 g fiber, 4 g pro. Exchanges: 1 starch, 1 carb., 1 fat. Carb choices: 2.

Bowl Game
Snack Mix

Mango-
Strawberry
Smoothie
recipe on page 131

Bowl Game Snack Mix

A light misting of nonstick cooking spray helps the taco seasoning mix cling to the crunchy popcorn.

SERVINGS 8 (¾ cup each)

CARB. PER SERVING 15 g

　5　cups air-popped popcorn
　　　Nonstick cooking spray
1½　teaspoons taco seasoning mix
　½　cup peanuts
　½　cup golden raisins
　¼　cup toasted pumpkin seeds

1. Remove uncooked kernels from popped corn. Place popped corn in a very large bowl; lightly coat popcorn with nonstick cooking spray. Sprinkle popcorn with taco seasoning mix; stir lightly to coat. Stir in peanuts, raisins, and pumpkin seeds. Stir again before serving.

PER SERVING: 128 cal., 7 g total fat (1 g sat. fat), 0 mg chol., 93 mg sodium, 15 g carb., 2 g fiber, 4 g pro. Exchanges: 0.5 fruit, 0.5 starch, 1 fat. Carb choices: 1.

Caramel Popcorn

The popping is easy—two full-size bags of microwave popcorn will yield enough popcorn to make this crunchy sweet treat.

SERVINGS 11 (1 cup each)

CARB. PER SERVING 19 g or 9 g

　½　cup packed brown sugar*
　¼　cup granulated sugar*
　¼　cup tub-style 50% to 70% vegetable oil spread
　¼　teaspoon salt
1½　teaspoons vanilla
　12　cups popped light microwave popcorn

1. Preheat oven to 300°F. In a 4-quart Dutch oven, heat and stir the brown sugar, granulated sugar, vegetable oil spread, and salt over medium heat until just boiling and sugar is dissolved. Remove from heat. Stir in vanilla. Add popcorn and toss until coated.

2. Place coated popcorn in a shallow roasting pan. Bake, uncovered, for 15 minutes, stirring once. Transfer to a large piece of foil or a large roasting pan to cool.

*****SUGAR SUBSTITUTES:** Choose from Sweet'N Low Brown or Sugar Twin Granulated Brown to substitute for the brown sugar. Follow package directions to use product amount equivalent to ½ cup brown sugar. We do not recommend a substitute for the granulated sugar.

PER SERVING: 105 cal., 4 g total fat (1 g sat. fat), 0 mg chol., 139 mg sodium, 19 g carb., 1 g fiber, 1 g pro. Exchanges: 1 carb., 0.5 fat. Carb choices: 1.

PER SERVING WITH SUBSTITUTE: Same as above, except 67 cal., 9 g carb. Exchanges: 0.5 carb. Carb choices: 0.5.

Granola Parfaits

Tropical Fruit Pops

Apricot Yogurt Delight

Fast-Fuel Solutions

Keep your health in mind when you shop vending machines for snacks or hypoglycemia helpers.

1. **Low-carb satisfiers:** Although beef jerky, nuts, and seeds are low-carb pick-me-ups, beware of their sodium content and consider fat and calories.

2. **Fast fuel:** Baked, whole grain, and portion-controlled snacks are healthful options. Check the package for servings inside and how that number relates to carb (or starch) and fat servings in your meal plan.

3. **Low blood glucose:** If your blood glucose is below 70 mg/dl and glucose gel isn't handy, reach for 4 ounces sugary soda, 7 small hard candies, or 10 fruit snack pieces (about 15 grams of carbohydrate). Eat, wait 15 minutes, then retest.

4. **Not for blood glucose:** Diet sodas will not raise blood glucose. Chocolate candy bars contain carbs, but the fat delays their release into your system.

Tropical Fruit Pops

No fat, no cholesterol, and few carbs—
what more could you ask for in a kid-pleasing treat?

SERVINGS 12 to 14 (1 pop each)
CARB. PER SERVING 12 g

- 2 cups chopped mango (about 2 large)
- 1 8-ounce can crushed pineapple (juice pack), undrained
- 1 medium banana, sliced
- ¼ cup frozen orange juice concentrate, thawed
- ¼ teaspoon ground ginger

1. In a blender, combine mango, undrained pineapple, banana, orange juice concentrate, and ginger. Blend until smooth. Divide fruit mixture among 12 to 14 compartments of freezer pop molds. (Or pour into 3-ounce paper or plastic cups. Cover cups with foil. With a sharp knife, make a slit in the foil of each. Add sticks for handles.) Freeze for 3 hours or until firm.

PER SERVING: 47 cal., 0 g total fat, 0 mg chol., 1 mg sodium, 12 g carb., 1 g fiber, 0 g pro. Exchanges: 1 fruit. Carb choices: 1.

Granola Parfaits

For on-the-go snacks, assemble these layered delights
in small plastic containers with lids and pack them in
a cooler with an ice pack.

SERVINGS 2 (1 parfait each)
CARB. PER SERVING 20 g

- ⅓ cup regular rolled oats
- 1 tablespoon pecan pieces or sliced almonds
- 1 teaspoon flaxseeds or flaxseed meal
- 1 6-ounce carton desired flavor fat-free yogurt with artificial sweetener
- 4 teaspoons desired flavor sugar-free or low sugar jam or preserves

1. Place a small skillet over medium-high heat. Add rolled oats, nuts, and flaxseeds to the skillet. Cook and stir for 45 to 60 seconds or until mixture is lightly toasted. Remove skillet from heat.

2. In each of two juice glassess, spoon one-fourth of the yogurt. Top each with one-fourth of the oat mixture and 1 teaspoon of the jam. Repeat layers.

PER SERVING: 139 cal., 4 g total fat (0 g sat. fat), 2 mg chol., 50 mg sodium, 20 g carb., 3 g fiber, 6 g pro. Exchanges: 0.5 milk, 1 starch, 0.5 fat. Carb choices: 1.

Apricot Yogurt Delight

Don't think you have time to make a healthful snack?
Try this four-ingredient special—it's quick as a wink.

SERVINGS 2 (about ¾ cup each)
CARB. PER SERVING 13 g

- 1 cup fat-free or low-fat Greek-style plain yogurt
- ¼ cup chopped fresh or dried apricots
- 2 tablespoons low-sugar apricot preserves
- 4 teaspoons chopped walnuts, toasted

1. Divide yogurt between two serving bowls. Top with apricots, preserves, and walnuts. Serve immediately.

PER SERVING: 126 cal., 3 g total fat (0 g sat. fat), 0 mg chol., 44 mg sodium, 13 g carb., 1 g fiber, 11 g pro. Exchanges: 0.5 milk, 0.5 carb., 0.5 fat. Carb choices: 1.

Mango-Strawberry Smoothie

Tofu adds both protein and body to this fruity blender
drink. Sip one when you hit a between-meal slump.
Pictured on page 129.

SERVINGS 3 (8 ounces each)
CARB. PER SERVING 30 g

- 1½ cups chilled orange juice
- ½ of a 12.3-ounce package light silken tofu, chilled and drained
- 1 medium mango, pitted, peeled, and cut up (about 1 cup)
- 1 cup frozen unsweetened whole strawberries
- Halved fresh strawberries (optional)

1. In a blender, combine orange juice, tofu, mango, and the 1 cup strawberries. Cover and blend until smooth. If desired, for garnish, thread fresh strawberry halves on three small skewers. Add a skewer to each serving. Serve immediately.

PER SERVING: 142 cal., 1 g total fat (0 g sat. fat), 0 mg chol., 52 mg sodium, 30 g carb., 2 g fiber, 5 g pro. Exchanges: 2 fruit, 0.5 lean meat. Carb choices: 2.

delightful desserts

Sometimes you need a little something to feed a craving. Even with diabetes, you can enjoy the sweet goodness of dessert if you choose wisely. Try one of these lightened-up favorites, each designed especially for you.

Peach-Blueberry Ginger-Oat Crisp

Take a bite of this irresistible crisp and you'll discover that the ginger in both the fruit and crust makes the flavor of summer-fresh peaches pop.

SERVINGS 8 (about ½ cup each)
CARB. PER SERVING 29 g or 24 g

- 4 cups sliced fresh peaches or frozen unsweetened peach slices, thawed and undrained
- 3 tablespoons packed brown sugar*
- 2 tablespoons all-purpose flour
- ½ teaspoon ground ginger
- 1 cup fresh or frozen unsweetened blueberries, thawed
- ¼ cup water
- 8 gingersnaps
- ⅔ cup quick-cooking rolled oats
- ¼ cup chopped pecans (optional)
- 2 tablespoons butter, melted
- 1 cup frozen light whipped dessert topping, thawed (optional)

1. Preheat oven to 375°F. In a large bowl, toss together peach slices, brown sugar, flour, and ginger. Add blueberries and the water; toss to combine. Spoon fruit mixture into a 2-quart square baking dish. Bake, uncovered, for 20 minutes.

2. Meanwhile, place gingersnaps in a heavy resealable plastic bag; seal bag. Using the flat side of a meat mallet or a rolling pin, crush cookies into ¼- to ½-inch pieces. Transfer cookies to a medium bowl. Stir in rolled oats and, if desired, chopped pecans. Stir in butter until well mixed. Sprinkle over partially baked fruit mixture.

3. Bake for 15 to 20 minutes more or until fruit is bubbly and topping is lightly browned. Cool on a wire rack for 30 minutes. Serve warm. If desired, top with whipped topping.

*SUGAR SUBSTITUTES: Choose from Sweet'N Low Brown or Sugar Twin Granulated Brown. Follow package directions to use product amount equivalent to 3 tablespoons brown sugar.

PER SERVING: 153 cal., 4 g total fat (2 g sat. fat), 8 mg chol., 68 mg sodium, 29 g carb., 3 g fiber, 2 g pro. Exchanges: 0.5 fruit, 1.5 carb., 1 fat. Carb choices: 2.
PER SERVING WITH SUBSTITUTE: Same as above, except 134 cal., 24 g carb., 67 mg sodium. Exchanges: 1 carb. Carb choices: 1.5.

Berry Ginger Shortcakes

Flaky, tender biscuits layered with ginger-accented fruit and a sour cream topping—a fabulous way to end a meal!

SERVINGS 10 (1 filled cake each)
CARB. PER SERVING 30 g

3	cups fresh blueberries, raspberries, blackberries, and/or sliced strawberries
2	tablespoons finely chopped crystallized ginger
1²⁄₃	cups all-purpose flour
1	tablespoon granulated sugar
2	teaspoons baking powder
¼	teaspoon baking soda
3	tablespoons butter
½	cup buttermilk
¼	cup refrigerated or frozen egg product, thawed, or 1 egg
½	of an 8-ounce container frozen light whipped dessert topping, thawed
¼	cup fat-free or light sour cream
	Sifted powdered sugar (optional)

1. In a small bowl, combine berries and ginger. Set aside.

2. Preheat oven to 425°F. For shortcakes: In a medium bowl, stir together flour, granulated sugar, baking powder, and baking soda. Using a pastry blender, cut in butter until mixture resembles coarse crumbs. Make a well in center of flour mixture. In a small bowl, combine buttermilk and egg. Add to flour mixture all at once, stirring just until moistened.

3. Lightly coat a baking sheet with *nonstick cooking spray*; set aside. On a lightly floured surface, pat dough to ½-inch thickness. Using a floured 2½-inch star-shape cookie cutter or a round biscuit cutter, cut dough into star shapes or rounds, rerolling scraps as necessary. Place on prepared baking sheet. Bake for 8 to 10 minutes or until golden. Cool slightly on a wire rack.

4. Meanwhile, in a small bowl, combine whipped topping and sour cream. Split shortcakes in half. Place bottoms on plates. Spoon berry mixture and whipped topping mixture over bottoms. Re-place shortcake tops. If desired, sprinkle with powdered sugar.

PER SERVING: 183 cal., 5 g total fat (4 g sat. fat), 11 mg chol., 186 mg sodium, 30 g carb., 2 g fiber, 4 g pro. Exchanges: 0.5 fruit, 1.5 carb., 1 fat. Carb choices: 2.

Strawberry-Rhubarb Crisp

In the spring and early summer, make this low-fat crisp with rhubarb and strawberries. Later in the summer, substitute ripe peaches.

SERVINGS 6 to 8
CARB. PER SERVING 26 g

⅓	cup low-sugar strawberry preserves
⅛	teaspoon ground cinnamon or nutmeg
2	cups sliced fresh strawberries
2	cups sliced fresh rhubarb
3	tablespoons all-purpose flour
½	cup quick-cooking rolled oats
2	tablespoons cornmeal
2	tablespoons honey
1	teaspoon vanilla

1. Preheat oven to 375°F. In a bowl, combine preserves and cinnamon. Add berries and rhubarb; stir gently to coat. Add flour; stir gently until combined. Spoon into a 9-inch pie plate. Bake, uncovered, for 20 minutes.

2. Meanwhile, in a bowl, combine oats and cornmeal. Stir in honey and vanilla until combined. Sprinkle over strawberry mixture. Bake, uncovered, for 20 minutes or until topping is golden and fruit is tender and bubbly. Cool about 20 minutes before serving. Serve warm.

PER SERVING: 117 cal., 1 g total fat (0 g sat. fat), 0 mg chol., 7 mg sodium, 26 g carb., 3 g fiber, 2 g pro. Exchanges: 0.5 fruit, 1 carb. Carb choices: 2.

PEACH CRISP: Prepare as above, except substitute low-sugar apricot preserves for strawberry preserves and 4 cups peeled and sliced fresh peaches for berries and rhubarb. Stir 2 teaspoons lemon juice into preserves.

PER SERVING: 142 cal., 1 g total fat (0 g sat. fat), 0 mg chol., 2 mg sodium, 33 g carb., 3 g fiber, 2 g pro. Exchanges: 1 fruit; 1 carb. Carb choices: 2.

Berry Ginger Shortcakes

Strawberry-Rhubarb Crisp

Raspberry-Lemonade Shortcakes

A slimmed-down version of classic hot milk sponge cake makes this raspberry variation of a summertime favorite low in calories and fat, yet oh, so luscious.

SERVINGS 12 (1 filled cake each)

CARB. PER SERVING 35 g or 29 g

2	eggs
1	cup all-purpose flour
1	teaspoon baking powder
1	teaspoon finely shredded lemon peel
¾	cup sugar*
½	cup fat-free milk
2	tablespoons tub-style 60% to 70% vegetable oil spread
1	recipe Raspberry-Lemonade Sauce (page 137)
	Small lemon wedges (optional)

1. Allow eggs to stand at room temperature for 30 minutes. Meanwhile, grease a 9×9×2-inch baking pan. Line pan with waxed paper. Grease and flour waxed paper; set pan aside. In a small bowl, stir together flour, baking powder, and lemon peel; set aside.

2. Preheat oven to 350°F. In a medium bowl, beat eggs with an electric mixer on high speed about 4 minutes or until thick. Gradually add sugar, beating on medium speed for 4 to 5 minutes or until light and fluffy. Add flour mixture; beat on low to medium speed just until combined.

3. In a small saucepan, heat and stir milk and vegetable oil spread until spread melts; add to batter, beating until combined. Pour batter into prepared pan.

4. Bake for 20 to 25 minutes or until a toothpick inserted near center comes out clean. Cool cake in pan on wire rack for 10 minutes. Invert cake onto wire rack lined with waxed paper; carefully peel off top waxed paper and cool completely.

5. Cut cake into 12 pieces. Split each cake piece in half horizontally. Place cake piece bottoms on individual dessert plates. Spoon half of the Raspberry-Lemonade Sauce over cake bottoms. Top with cake piece tops. Spoon remaining sauce onto cakes. If desired, garnish with lemon wedges.

*SUGAR SUBSTITUTES: Choose Splenda Sugar Blend for Baking. Follow package directions to use product amount equivalent to ¾ cup sugar.

RASPBERRY-LEMONADE SAUCE: Place 3 cups fresh or frozen raspberries in a medium bowl. (Thaw frozen raspberries, if using, in the bowl; do not drain.) Mash berries with a potato masher. In a small saucepan, combine ⅓ cup sugar,** ¾ teaspoon cornstarch, and ½ teaspoon finely shredded lemon peel. Add mashed raspberries. Cook and stir until thickened and bubbly; cook and stir for 2 minutes more. Remove from heat. Cool about 10 minutes. Stir in 4 cups fresh or frozen (thawed and drained) raspberries.

**SUGAR SUBSTITUTES: We do not recommend sugar substitutes for the sauce.

PER SERVING: 175 cal., 3 g total fat (1 g sat. fat), 35 mg chol., 49 mg sodium, 35 g carb., 5 g fiber, 3 g pro. Exchanges: 0.5 fruit, 2 carb. Carb choices: 2.

PER SERVING WITH SUGAR SUBSTITUTE: Same as above, except 156 cal., 29 g carb. Exchanges: 1.5 carb.

Berry Pudding Cakes

Berry Pudding Cakes

Sugar is a must for this popoverlike berry dessert. Sugar substitutes don't give the same appealing texture.

SERVINGS 6 (1 cake each)

CARB. PER SERVING 26 g

---

2 eggs, lightly beaten
¼ cup granulated sugar
1 teaspoon vanilla
Dash salt
1 cup fat-free milk
½ cup all-purpose flour
½ teaspoon baking powder
3 cups fresh berries (such as raspberries, blueberries, and/or sliced strawberries)
2 teaspoons powdered sugar (optional)

1. Preheat oven to 400°F. Lightly coat six 6-ounce individual quiche dishes with *nonstick cooking spray.* Arrange in a 15×10×1-inch baking pan; set aside. In a medium bowl, combine eggs, granulated sugar, vanilla, and salt; whisk until light and frothy. Whisk in milk until combined. Add flour and baking powder; whisk until smooth.

2. Divide berries among prepared quiche dishes. Pour batter over berries. (Batter will not cover berries completely.) Bake about 20 minutes or until puffed and golden brown. Serve warm. If desired, sift powdered sugar over each serving.

PER SERVING: 141 cal., 2 g total fat (1 g sat. fat), 71 mg chol., 86 mg sodium, 26 g carb., 3 g fiber, 5 g pro. Exchanges: 0.5 fruit, 1.5 carb. Carb choices: 2.

Mocha Angel Cake
with Chai-Spiced Cream

Mocha Angel Cake with Chai-Spiced Cream

Savor the flavors of both coffee and tea at once in this tempting dessert. Espresso coffee powder gives the cake a rich mocha flavor, and the creamy topper boasts six spices that commonly season chai, the Indian tea drink.

SERVINGS 12 (1 wedge each)
CARB. PER SERVING 26 g

1¼   cups egg whites (8 to 10 large)
¾   cup sifted cake flour or sifted all-purpose flour
½   cup powdered sugar
¼   cup unsweetened cocoa powder
1   tablespoon instant espresso coffee powder or crushed instant coffee crystals
1¼   teaspoons cream of tartar
½   teaspoon vanilla
⅔   cup granulated sugar*
1   recipe Chai-Spiced Cream (page 139)
12   chocolate-covered coffee beans (optional)

1. In a very large bowl, let egg whites stand at room temperature for 30 minutes. Meanwhile, sift flour, powdered sugar, cocoa powder, and espresso powder together three times; set aside.

2. Adjust baking rack to lowest position in oven. Preheat oven to 350°F. Add cream of tartar and vanilla to egg whites. Beat on medium speed until soft peaks form (tips curl). Gradually add granulated sugar, about 2 tablespoons at a time, beating until stiff peaks form (tips stand straight). Sift about one-fourth of the flour mixture over beaten egg whites. Fold in gently. Repeat, folding in remaining flour mixture by thirds. Spoon into an ungreased 10-inch tube pan. Using a table knife, gently cut through batter to remove any air pockets.

3. Bake for 30 to 35 minutes or until top springs back when lightly touched. Immediately invert cake in pan; let stand until completely cool. Loosen side of cake from pan; remove cake.

4. Spoon Chai-Spiced Cream in mounds around top of cake. If desired, top each mound with a coffee bean.

CHAI-SPICED CREAM: Place half of an 8-ounce container frozen light whipped dessert topping, thawed, in a bowl. Fold in 1/8 teaspoon each ground cardamom and ground cinnamon and a dash each ground cloves, ground nutmeg, ground black pepper, and ground ginger.

*SUGAR SUBSTITUTES: We do not recommend sugar substitutes for this recipe.

PER SERVING: 137 cal., 1 g total fat (1 g sat. fat), 0 mg chol., 43 mg sodium, 26 g carb., 0 g fiber, 4 g pro. Exchanges: 1.5 carb. Carb choices: 2.

Coconut-Blueberry Cheesecake Bars

If you like cheesecake, you're going to love these bursting-with-berries bars.

SERVINGS about 32 (1 bar each)
CARB. PER SERVING 11 g or 7 g

- 1/3 cup butter
- 3/4 cup finely crushed graham crackers
- 1/2 cup all-purpose flour
- 1/2 cup flaked coconut
- 1/2 cup ground pecans
- 1/4 cup sugar*
- 1 1/2 8-ounce packages reduced-fat cream cheese (Neufchâtel), softened
- 1/2 cup sugar*
- 1 cup refrigerated or frozen egg product, thawed, or 4 eggs, lightly beaten
- 1 tablespoon brandy or fat-free milk
- 1 teaspoon vanilla
- 2 cups blueberries

1. Preheat oven to 350°F. Lightly grease a 13×9×2-inch baking pan; set aside. For crust: In a small saucepan, heat butter over medium heat until the color of light brown sugar. Remove from heat; set aside. In a medium bowl, stir together graham crackers, flour, coconut, pecans, and the 1/4 cup sugar. Stir in butter until combined. Evenly press on bottom of prepared pan. Bake for 8 to 10 minutes or until lightly browned.

2. Meanwhile, in a bowl, beat cream cheese and the 1/2 cup sugar on medium speed until combined. Add eggs, brandy, and vanilla. Beat until combined. Pour over hot crust. Sprinkle with blueberries.

3. Bake for 18 to 20 minutes or until center appears set. Cool in pan on a wire rack. Cover and chill. Cut into bars. Store, covered, in refrigerator.

QUICK TIP ◖
Use a long sharp knife to cut through cheesecake bars, wiping the knife clean with wet paper towels between cuts.

Coconut-Blueberry Cheesecake Bars

*SUGAR SUBSTITUTES: Choose from Splenda granular or Sweet'N Low bulk or packets. Follow package directions to use product amount equivalent to 1/4 cup or 1/2 cup sugar.

PER SERVING: 109 cal., 6 g total fat (3 g sat. fat), 13 mg chol., 79 mg sodium, 11 g carb., 1 g fiber, 2 g pro. Exchanges: 1 carb., 1 fat. Carb choices: 1.

PER SERVING WITH SUBSTITUTE: Same as above, except 93 cal., 7 g carb. Exchanges: 0.5 carb. Carb choices: 0.5.

Fresh Fruit Tart

Fresh Fruit Tart

Showcase your favorite summer fruits within this refreshing tart's layers of lightly sweetened sour cream and toasted coconut. Offer glasses of unsweetened iced tea or sugar-free lemonade as thirst-quenching serve-alongs.

SERVINGS 12 (1 wedge each)
CARB. PER SERVING 17 g

- 1 recipe Single-Crust Pastry (below)
- 1 8-ounce carton fat-free or light sour cream
- 2 tablespoons sugar
- ⅓ cup shredded coconut, toasted
- 2 to 3 cups assorted fresh fruit (such as sliced peaches, sliced strawberries, blueberries, raspberries, pitted dark sweet cherries, sliced bananas, and/or sliced mango)

1. Preheat oven to 450°F. Prepare Single-Crust Pastry. On a lightly floured surface, flatten dough ball with your hands. Roll dough from center to edge into a circle about 11 inches in diameter. To transfer pastry, wrap it around the rolling pin. Unroll pastry into a 9-inch tart pan with a removable bottom, being careful not to stretch pastry. Press pastry into fluted side of tart pan. Trim pastry to the edge of the tart pan. Prick the bottom and side of pastry generously with the tines of a fork.
2. Bake for 10 to 12 minutes or until pastry is golden. Cool in pan on a wire rack.
3. In a small bowl, stir together sour cream and sugar; spread over cooled crust. Cover and chill for up to 2 hours. To serve, sprinkle with half of the coconut; arrange fruit on top. Sprinkle with remaining coconut. Cut into 12 wedges

SINGLE-CRUST PASTRY: In a large bowl, stir together 1¼ cups all-purpose flour and ¼ teaspoon salt. Using a pastry blender, cut in ⅓ cup shortening until pieces are pea size. Sprinkle 1 tablespoon cold water over part of the mixture; gently toss with a fork. Push moistened dough to the side of the bowl. Repeat moistening dough, using 1 tablespoon cold water at a time, until all of the dough is moistened (4 to 5 tablespoons cold water total). Form dough into a ball.

PER SERVING: 138 cal., 7 g total fat (3 g sat. fat), 2 mg chol., 86 mg sodium, 17 g carb., 1 g fiber, 2 g pro. Exchanges: 1 carb., 1 fat. Carb choices: 1.

Grape Crepes

Crème de cassis is a liqueur with a delicate black currant flavor.

SERVINGS 8 (1 crepe each)
CARB. PER SERVING 14 g or 13 g

- ½ cup fat-free milk
- ⅓ cup white whole wheat flour or all-purpose flour
- ¼ cup refrigerated or frozen egg product, thawed, or 1 egg, lightly beaten
- 1 teaspoon canola oil
- ⅛ teaspoon salt
- 3 cups seedless red grapes, halved
- 3 tablespoons crème de cassis or grape juice
- 2 tablespoons water
- 1 teaspoon cornstarch
- ½ cup light sour cream
- 1 tablespoon sugar*

1. For crepe batter: In a medium bowl, whisk together milk, flour, egg, oil, and salt until smooth.
2. Lightly oil a 7- to 8-inch nonstick skillet with flared side. Heat over medium-high heat. Remove from heat. Spoon in about 2 tablespoons of the crepe batter; lift and tilt skillet to spread batter. Return to heat; cook until top is set and dry (30 to 45 seconds). (Or cook on a crepe maker according to manufacturer's directions.) Invert skillet over paper towels; remove crepe. Repeat with remaining batter to make 8 crepes, oiling skillet occasionally. Set crepes aside.
3. In a large skillet, combine grapes, crème de cassis, the water, and cornstarch. Cook and stir until mixture just comes to boiling; reduce heat. Cook and stir for 4 to 6 minutes more or until grapes are softened but still hold their shape and mixture is slightly thickened.
4. In a small bowl, combine sour cream and sugar. To serve, spread unbrowned sides of crepes with sour cream mixture. Fold crepes as desired. Top with grape mixture.

***SUGAR SUBSTITUTES:** Choose from Splenda granular, Sweet'N Low bulk or packets, or Equal spoonful or packets. Follow package directions to use product amount equivalent to 1 tablespoon sugar.

PER SERVING: 86 cal., 2 g total fat (1 g sat. fat), 5 mg chol., 67 mg sodium, 14 g carb., 1 g fiber, 3 g pro. Exchanges: 0.5 fruit, 0.5 starch, 0.5 fat. Carb choices: 1.
PER SERVING WITH SUGAR SUBSTITUTE: Same as above, except 81 cal., 13 g carb.

Pineapple-Berry Hobo Pack

Spiff up the presentation of this fruity dessert by serving the mixture in a cut-glass bowl.

SERVINGS 4 (¾ cup each)

CARB. PER SERVING 18 g

- 2 cups coarsely chopped, cored fresh pineapple, peeled if desired
- 1 tablespoon packed brown sugar
- 1 teaspoon chopped crystallized ginger
- 1 cup raspberries and/or blueberries
- 1 teaspoon Demerara sugar or brown sugar

1. Fold a 36×18-inch piece of heavy foil in half to make an 18-inch square. Place pineapple in center of foil. Sprinkle with brown sugar and ginger. Bring up two opposite edges of foil; seal with a double fold. Fold remaining edges to completely enclose pineapple, leaving space for steam to build.

2. For a charcoal grill, place packet on the grill rack directly over medium coals. Grill, uncovered, about 10 minutes or until hot, turning occasionally. (For a gas grill, preheat grill. Reduce heat to medium. Place packet on grill rack over heat. Cover and grill as above.)

3. Carefully open packet. Add berries and sprinkle with Demerara sugar.

PER SERVING: 72 cal., 0 g total fat, 0 mg chol., 3 mg sodium, 18 g carb., 3 g fiber, 1 g pro. Exchanges: 1 fruit. Carb choices: 1.

Roasted Mango with Coconut Topping

Pineapple-Berry Hobo Pack

Roasted Mango with Coconut Topping

The simple topping creates a spicy, candylike coating.

SERVINGS 2 (¾ cup each)
CARB. PER SERVING 20 g

- 1 medium ripe mango, seeded, peeled, and cubed
- 1 tablespoon flaked coconut
- 1 teaspoon finely shredded orange peel
- 1 teaspoon finely chopped crystallized ginger

1. Preheat oven to 350°F. Place mango in two 6-ounce custard cups. For topping: Combine coconut, orange peel, and ginger. Sprinkle topping over mango. Bake about 10 minutes or just until topping begins to brown.

Zucchini-Banana Snack Cake

PER SERVING: 89 cal., 2 g total fat (1 g sat. fat), 0 mg chol., 14 mg sodium, 20 g carb., 2 g fiber, 1 g pro. Exchanges: 1 fruit. Carb choices: 1.

Zucchini-Banana Snack Cake

Keep a secret—these chocolatey, brownielike cake squares are filled with good-for-you ingredients.

SERVINGS 24 (1 piece each)
CARB. PER SERVING 16 g or 13 g

- Nonstick cooking spray
- 1 cup all-purpose flour
- 1 cup whole wheat flour
- ¼ cup flaxseed meal or wheat germ
- ¼ cup unsweetened cocoa powder
- 2 teaspoons baking powder
- ½ teaspoon salt
- ½ cup refrigerated or frozen egg product, thawed, or 2 eggs, slightly beaten
- ¾ cup sugar*
- ½ cup canola oil
- ⅓ cup fat-free milk
- 1 cup peeled (if desired) and shredded zucchini
- 1 medium-size ripe banana, mashed (½ cup)
- ½ cup miniature semisweet chocolate pieces (optional)

1. Preheat oven to 350°F. Lightly coat a 13×9×2-inch baking pan with nonstick cooking spray; set aside. In a large bowl, combine all-purpose flour, whole wheat flour, flaxseed meal or wheat germ, cocoa powder, baking powder, and salt. Make a well in center of flour mixture; set aside.

2. In a medium bowl, whisk together eggs, sugar, canola oil, and milk until well mixed. Stir in zucchini and banana. Add zucchini mixture all at once to flour mixture. Stir just until moistened. Fold in chocolate pieces. Pour batter into prepared pan, spreading evenly.

3. Bake 20 to 25 minutes or until top springs back when lightly touched. Cool completely on a wire rack. Cut into 24 pieces.

*SUGAR SUBSTITUTES: Choose Splenda Sugar Blend for Baking. Follow package directions to use product amount equivalent to ¾ cup sugar.

PER SERVING: 118 cal., 5 g total fat (0 g sat. fat), 0 mg chol., 80 mg sodium, 16 g carb., 1 g fiber, 2 g pro. Exchanges: 1 carb., 1 fat. Carb choices: 1.

PER SERVING WITH SUBSTITUTE: Same as above, except 109 cal., 13 g carb.

Chocolate Cookie Treats

For easy drizzling, spoon the glaze into a heavy resealable plastic bag, snip a corner, and gently squeeze.

SERVINGS about 32 (1 cookie each)

CARB. PER SERVING 14 g or 11 g

- 1 ounce sweet baking, bittersweet, or semisweet chocolate, melted and cooled slightly
- 5 tablespoons butter, softened
- ¾ cup granulated sugar*
- 1 large egg
- 1 egg yolk
- 1 teaspoon vanilla
- 1⅓ cups all-purpose flour
- ⅓ cup walnuts, finely chopped
- 32 walnut halves
- 1 recipe Chocolate Glaze (right)
  Powdered sugar (optional)

1. Preheat oven to 350°F. Line cookie sheets with parchment paper; set aside. While chocolate cools, in a medium bowl, beat butter on medium-high speed about 2 minutes or until smooth. Add granulated sugar, beating until creamy. Add egg, egg yolk, and vanilla, beating well. Stir in melted chocolate. Stir in flour and chopped walnuts. Cover and chill for 1 hour.

2. Shape dough into 1-inch balls. Place balls 2 inches apart on prepared cookie sheets. Press a walnut half into top of each cookie. Bake for 10 to 12 minutes or until centers are set. Transfer cookies to a wire rack to cool.

3. Spoon Chocolate Glaze evenly over cooled cookies. Let stand until glaze is set. If desired, sprinkle with powdered sugar. Store the cookies in an airtight container between layers of waxed paper for up to 1 week or freeze for up to 1 month.

CHOCOLATE GLAZE: In a small saucepan, melt 1 ounce sweet baking, bittersweet, or semisweet chocolate and 1 tablespoon butter over low heat. Remove from heat. Add ¼ teaspoon vanilla, 1 cup powdered sugar, and 2 tablespoons fat-free milk. Stir until well combined.

*SUGAR SUBSTITUTES: Choose Splenda Sugar Blend for Baking. Follow package directions to use product amount equivalent to ¾ cup sugar.

PER SERVING: 99 cal., 5 g total fat (2 g sat. fat), 19 mg chol., 19 mg sodium, 14 g carb., 0 g fiber, 1 g pro. Exchanges: 1 carb., 1 fat. Carb choices: 1.

PER SERVING WITH SUBSTITUTE: Same as above, except 92 cal., 11 g carb.

Almond Sandwich Cookies

These lacy cookies spread while baking, so be sure to place dough at least 3 inches apart on the cookie sheet.

SERVINGS about 30 (1 sandwich cookie each)

CARB. PER SERVING 14 g or 11 g

- 1 cup rolled oats
- ¾ cup sugar*
- 2 tablespoons all-purpose flour
- 1 teaspoon ground cardamom
- ¼ teaspoon salt
- ¼ teaspoon baking powder
- ¼ cup refrigerated or frozen egg product, thawed, or 1 egg, lightly beaten
- ½ cup butter, melted
- 1 teaspoon vanilla
- 1 cup slivered almonds
- 1 recipe Vanilla Cream (below)

1. Preheat oven to 325°F. Line a cookie sheet with foil and lightly coat foil with *nonstick cooking spray;* set aside.

2. In a large mixing bowl, combine oats, sugar, flour, cardamom, salt, and baking powder. In a medium bowl, whisk together egg, butter, and vanilla until well combined. Add egg mixture to oat mixture; stir until well combined. Add the almonds and stir until evenly distributed.

3. Drop level teaspoons of dough 3 inches apart on prepared cookie sheet. Bake for 10 to 12 minutes or until edges are browned. Let cookies cool completely, then peel from foil. Repeat with remaining dough.

4. For each sandwich cookie, spread bottom side of a cookie with a rounded teaspoon of Vanilla Cream. Place another cookie, top side up, on top of filling.

VANILLA CREAM: In a large mixing bowl, beat ¼ cup butter, softened, with 1 cup powdered sugar until smooth. Beat in 1 teaspoon vanilla. Gradually beat in an additional ½ cup powdered sugar until mixture is smooth.

*SUGAR SUBSTITUTES: Choose Splenda Sugar Blend for Baking. Follow package directions to use product amount equivalent to ¾ cup sugar.

PER SERVING: 118 cal., 7 g total fat (3 g sat. fat), 12 mg chol., 58 mg sodium, 14 g carb., 1 g fiber, 1 g pro. Exchanges: 1 carb., 1.5 fat. Carb choices: 1.

PER SERVING WITH SUBSTITUTE: Same as above, except 111 cal., 11 g carb.

Raspberry Meringues

Raspberry jam gives these light and airy cookies a tangy kick.

SERVINGS about 20 (1 cookie each)

CARB. PER SERVING 5 g

- 2 egg whites
- 1 tablespoon low-sugar seedless red raspberry jam (at room temperature)
- 6 drops red food coloring
- ⅓ cup superfine sugar or granulated sugar
- ⅓ cup sifted powdered sugar
- ⅛ teaspoon cream of tartar

1. Let egg whites stand, covered, in a large glass mixing bowl at room temperature for 30 minutes. Meanwhile, line two large baking sheets with parchment paper.

2. Preheat oven to 300°F. In a small bowl, combine jam (at room temperature) and red food coloring. Set aside.

3. In a small bowl, combine sugars; set aside. Uncover eggs and add cream of tartar. Beat with an electric mixer on medium speed until soft peaks form (tips curl). Add sugar mixture, 1 tablespoon at a time, beating on medium speed for 5 to 7 minutes or until stiff glossy peaks form (tips stand straight) and sugar is dissolved.

4. Use a spatula to gently fold ½ cup of the meringue mixture into the jam, then gently fold jam mixture into the remaining meringue.

5. Using a pastry bag fitted with a large star tip, pipe the meringue in 2-inch free-form hearts or Xs and Os onto the parchment paper.

6. Place baking sheets in preheated oven. Turn off oven. Let meringues dry in oven, with door closed, for 1 hour or until dry and crisp but still light in color. Let cool on parchment paper. Gently remove meringues.

PER SERVING: 22 cal., 0 g total fat, 0 mg chol., 6 mg sodium, 5 g carb., 0 g fiber, 0 g pro. Exchanges: Carb choices: 0.

For a flash of fruit flavor, sandwich your favorite fruit sorbet or sherbet between these crispy cookie wafers.

Ice Cream Sandwiches

Ice Cream Sandwiches

For ease, dip the ice cream scoop in warm water between each ice cream ball.

SERVINGS 13 (1 sandwich each)
CARB. PER SERVING 19 g

¼ cup butter, softened
¼ cup sugar*
½ teaspoon baking powder
½ teaspoon vanilla
⅛ teaspoon salt
2 tablespoons refrigerated or frozen egg product, thawed, or 1 egg white
1¼ cups cake flour or all-purpose flour
2 cups low-fat or light chocolate, vanilla, or fudge nut sundae ice cream
½ cup chopped toasted almonds or pecans (optional)

1. Preheat oven to 375°F. In a small bowl, beat butter with an electric mixer on medium speed for 30 seconds. Add sugar, baking powder, vanilla, and salt; beat until combined. Add egg; beat until combined. Beat in as much of the flour as you can with the mixer. Using a wooden spoon, stir in any remaining flour (or knead gently until combined). Shape dough into a ball.
2. On a lightly floured surface, roll dough to ⅛-inch thickness. Using a 2-inch square or round cutter with scalloped edges, cut out dough. Place 1 inch apart on ungreased cookie sheets.
3. Bake for 6 to 8 minutes or until edges are very lightly browned. Transfer cookies to wire racks; let cool.
4. Meanwhile, scoop 13 ice cream balls, about 2 tablespoons each. Place ice cream balls on a waxed paper-lined baking sheet and place in the freezer until ready to assemble sandwiches.
5. To assemble, remove a few ice cream balls at a time. Place 1 ice cream ball on a cookie. Top with a second cookie, pressing gently together. Repeat with remaining ice cream balls and cookies. If desired, sprinkle nuts onto edges of ice cream and press in gently so nuts stick.
6. Place sandwiches on a waxed paper-lined baking sheet. Freeze for 3 hours or until firm. To store, freeze for up to 2 weeks in resealable plastic bags.
***SUGAR SUBSTITUTES:** We do not recommend sugar substitutes for this recipe.
PER SERVING: 126 cal., 5 g total fat (3 g sat. fat), 12 mg chol., 78 mg sodium, 19 g carb., 1 g fiber, 2 g pro. Exchanges: 1 carb., 1 fat. Carb choices: 1.

Melon-Mango
Ice Cream

Melon-Mango Ice Cream

Making your own ice cream is especially fun when it's this tropical pleaser. It won't derail your diabetes meal plan because it's made with fat-free half-and-half and buttermilk instead of whipping cream.

SERVINGS 24 (½ cup each)
CARB. PER SERVING 15 g

    2 cups whole milk
    2 cups buttermilk
    2 cups fat-free half-and-half
    1 cup sugar*
    1 tablespoon vanilla
  1½ cups chopped cantaloupe
  1½ cups chopped mango
       Edible flowers (optional)

1. In a large bowl, combine milk, buttermilk, fat-free half-and-half, sugar, and vanilla. Stir to dissolve sugar.
2. In a blender or food processor, combine cantaloupe and mango. Cover and blend or process until smooth. Stir pureed fruit into milk mixture. Freeze in a 4- to 5-quart ice cream freezer according to the manufacturer's directions. If desired, ripen for 4 hours.**

3. If desired, garnish individual servings with edible flowers.

*SUGAR SUBSTITUTES: We do not recommend sugar substitutes for this recipe.

**TEST KITCHEN TIP: Ripening homemade ice cream improves the texture and helps to keep it from melting too quickly while eating. To ripen in a traditional-style ice cream freezer, after churning, remove the lid and dasher and cover the top of the freezer can with waxed paper or foil. Plug the hole in the lid with a small piece of cloth; replace the lid. Pack the outer freezer bucket with enough ice and rock salt to cover the top of the freezer can (use 1 cup salt for each 4 cups ice). Ripen about 4 hours. When using an ice cream freezer with an insulated freezer bowl, transfer the ice cream to a covered freezer container and ripen by freezing it in your regular freezer about 4 hours (or check the manufacturer's recommendations).

PER SERVING: 76 cal., 1 g total fat (1 g sat. fat), 4 mg chol., 60 mg sodium, 15 g carb., 0 g fiber, 2 g pro. Exchanges: 1 carb. Carb choices: 1.

Pecan-Maple Sorbet Cups

Tuile" is French for tile. Traditionally these nutty, crisp cookies are shaped over a rolling pin or a mold so they set up to look like curved roofing tiles. In this recipe, the cookies are shaped in or over muffins cups and filled sorbet.

SERVINGS 10 (1 tuile and 2/3 cup sorbet each)
CARB. PER SERVING: 32 g

 2 egg whites
 1/2 cup ground pecans
 3 tablespoons butter, melted
 1/4 teaspoon maple flavoring
 1/2 cup sugar*
 1/2 cup all-purpose flour
 3 cups desired flavor sorbet (such as raspberry, lemon, and/or coconut)
   Fresh mint leaves (optional)

1. In a medium bowl, let egg whites stand at room temperature for 30 minutes.

2. Preheat oven to 375°F. Line large cookie sheets with foil or parchment paper. If using foil, lightly grease foil; set aside. In a small bowl, combine ground pecans, butter, and maple flavoring; set aside.

3. Beat egg whites with an electric mixer on medium speed until soft peaks form (tips curl). Gradually add sugar, beating on high speed until stiff peaks form (tips stand straight). Fold in about half of the flour. Gently stir in pecan mixture. Fold in the remaining flour until thoroughly combined.

4. For each tuile: Drop two rounded measuring tablespoons of the batter onto prepared cookie sheets; leave 4 inches between mounds (place only two or three mounds on each baking sheet). Using the back of a spoon, spread each mound into a 4-inch circle. If necessary, coat the back of the spoon with *nonstick cooking spray* to prevent sticking.

5. Bake for 5 to 7 minutes or until tuiles are golden brown around edges and centers are lightly browned. Using a wide spatula, immediately remove the tuiles and gently press each warm tuile into a 3 1/2-inch (jumbo) muffin cup, pleating sides as needed to form a cup. (Or wrap each warm tuile around the bottom of a 2 1/2-inch muffin cup, pleating sides as needed to form a cup.) Cool tuiles until they hold their shape. Carefully remove from muffin cups. Cool completely on a wire rack.

6. To serve, using a small ice cream scoop, scoop sorbet into tuile cups. If desired, garnish with mint leaves.

*SUGAR SUBSTITUTES: We do not recommend sugar substitutes for this recipe.
PER SERVING: 194 cal., 8 g total fat (3 g sat. fat), 9 mg chol., 42 mg sodium, 32 g carb., 1 g fiber, 2 g pro. Exchanges: 2 other carb., 1.5 fat. Carb choices: 2.

Watermelon-Berry Granita

All blueberries with the watermelon will give a purply red ice. Add all strawberries for a vivid red hue.

SERVINGS 10 (3/4 cup each)
CARB. PER SERVING 13 g or 8 g

 3/4 cup water
 1/3 cup sugar*
 3 cups seeded watermelon cubes
 2 cups blueberries and/or halved strawberries

1. In a small saucepan, combine the water and sugar (if using); bring to boiling, stirring until sugar is dissolved. Boil gently, uncovered, for 2 minutes. Remove from heat; cool slightly. If using a sugar substitute, combine water and sugar substitute in a small bowl; stir to dissolve. Do not heat.

2. Meanwhile, in a blender or large food processor, combine watermelon and berries. Cover and blend or process until nearly smooth. Add the sugar mixture; blend or process until smooth. Transfer to a 3-quart rectangular baking dish. Cover and freeze about 2 1/2 hours or until almost solid.

3. Remove mixture from freezer. Using a fork, break up the frozen mixture until almost smooth but not melted. Cover and freeze for 1 hour more.** Break up the frozen mixture with a fork and serve in paper cups or shallow bowls.

*SUGAR SUBSTITUTES: Choose from Splenda granular, Equal packets, Equal Spoonful, Sweet'N Low packets or bulk. Be sure to use package directions to determine product amount equivalent to 1/3 cup sugar.
**TEST KITCHEN TIP: If mixture is frozen longer than the final hour, let it stand at room temperature about 20 minutes before breaking up mixture with a fork and serving.
PER SERVING: 52 cal., 0 g total fat, 0 mg chol., 1 mg sodium, 13 g carb., 2 g fiber, 0 g pro. Exchanges: 0.5 other carb., 0.5 fruit. Carb choices: 1.
PER SERVING WITH SUBSTITUTE: Same as above, except 33 cal., 8 g carb. Carb choice: 0.5.

Pecan-Maple
Sorbet Cups

Watermelon-Berry Granita

Fix-Fast Desserts

When you deserve a little sweet reward, dish up one of these easy-to-make treats.

1. **Pop plump and juicy grapes** in the freezer. Grab a handful for a sweet treat.

2. **Scoop up** a ball or two of fruit sorbet.

3. **Reach for a sugar-free** frozen pop stick.

4. **Lightly drizzle** chocolate ice cream topping over sliced banana.

5. **Lift the lid** on a single-size serving of sugar-free vanilla pudding and use a couple of vanilla wafers as dippers.

6. **Sandwich** a small scoop of light or low-fat ice cream between two crisp chocolate wafer cookies.

7. **Place a spoonful** of thawed light whipped dessert topping in a fresh peach half and sprinkle with a few toasted almonds.

8. **Slice up** a small fresh pear or apple and dip in a little caramel ice cream topping.

managing your diabetes

Understanding diabetes gives you a better chance of controlling it and preventing complications. It pays to learn all you can, then develop a plan that fits your lifestyle.

An estimated 21 million people in the United States, or 7 percent of the U.S. population, have diabetes, according to the Centers for Disease Control and Prevention. An additional 54 million Americans have pre-diabetes, indicating an increased risk of developing diabetes. If you're one of them, remember that you—not your doctor, dietitian, or other health professional—play the most important role in staying healthy.

Define Your Diabetes
Your health care team will work with you to develop a personalized diabetes management plan, consisting of healthful foods, physical activity, and, if necessary, the medication that's right for you and your type of diabetes (type 1, type 2, or gestational).

Type 1 diabetes: In this type, the pancreas doesn't produce insulin, so people with type 1 diabetes must take insulin. Treatment typically begins with an individualized meal plan, guidelines for physical activity, and blood glucose testing. Insulin therapy is then planned around lifestyle and eating patterns.

Type 2 diabetes: In type 2 diabetes, either the pancreas doesn't produce enough insulin or the body doesn't properly respond to insulin, so too much glucose remains in the blood. Many people control type 2 diabetes by following a specially designed meal plan and engaging in regular physical activity. The right plan can help people reach and attain a desirable weight, plus healthy blood glucose, blood cholesterol, and blood pressure levels. As the disease progresses, treatment may expand to include oral medications, oral medications with insulin, or insulin alone.

Gestational diabetes: This type develops only during pregnancy. Women who've had gestational diabetes have a higher risk of developing type 2 diabetes.

Develop Your Meal Plan
Adhering to a healthful meal plan is one of the most important measures you can take to control your blood glucose. Work with a dietitian to design a meal plan that reflects your individual needs and preferences. Your meal plan should also:

- Include fruits, vegetables, and whole grains.
- Reduce the amount of saturated fat and cholesterol you eat.
- Minimize the amount of salt or sodium you eat.
- Incorporate a moderate amount of sugar, because some sugar can be part of a healthful diabetes meal plan.
- Help you maintain or achieve an ideal weight.

Follow Your Meal Plan
As you start following your meal plan, you'll see that it gives you some flexibility regarding what, how much, and when you eat, but you have to be comfortable with the foods it suggests. It will guide you in eating appropriate amounts of three major nutrients—carbohydrate, protein, and fat—at the right times. Your meal plan will be nutritionally balanced, allowing you to get the vitamins, minerals, and fiber your body needs. And if you need to lose weight, it will indicate how many calories you should consume every day in order to lose the extra pounds at a realistic pace.

Your meal plan can be simple, especially if you use a proven technique to keep track of what you're eating. Two well-known meal-planning systems for diabetes are diabetic exchanges and carbohydrate counting. Your dietitian may suggest one or the other. To help you follow either system, every recipe in this book provides nutrition information, including the number of exchanges and carb choices in each serving. (Turn to *page 153* to see how to use this information.)

Track the Exchanges

Exchange Lists for Meal Planning outlines a system designed by the American Diabetes Association and the American Dietetic Association. To use the exchange system, your dietitian will work with you to develop a pattern of food exchanges—or a meal plan—suited to your specific needs. You'll be able to keep track of the number of exchanges from various food groups that you eat each day. Tally those numbers and match the total to the

daily allowance set in your meal plan. (For more information, see *diabetes.org*.)

Count Carbohydrates

Carbohydrate counting is the method many diabetes educators prefer for keeping tabs on what you eat. It makes sense because the carbohydrate content of foods has the greatest effect on blood glucose

levels. If you focus on carbohydrate, you can eat a variety of foods and still control your blood glucose.

When counting carbohydrate, you can tally the number of grams you eat each day. Or you can count the number of carbohydrate choices, which allows you to work with smaller numbers. We offer both numbers with our recipes.

Monitor Your Blood Glucose

Whether you have type 1 or type 2 diabetes, it's important to test your blood glucose, especially if you're taking insulin shots or oral medication. Usually you test blood glucose before each meal. Your health care providers will teach you how to measure your blood glucose with a simple finger-prick test, as well as how to adjust your food intake, physical activity, and/or medication when your blood glucose is too high or too low. Your health care providers will help you set blood glucose goals. For example, the American Diabetes Association suggests a target for fasting or before meals is 90 to 130 milligrams/deciliter. At two hours after the start of a meal, the goal is less than 180 milligrams/deciliter. Your A1C level (the average amount of glucose in the blood over the last few months) should be less than 7.0 percent. To keep your blood glucose at a healthy level, follow these five important guidelines:

- Eat about the same amount of food each day.
- Eat meals and snacks about the same times each day.
- Do not skip meals or snacks.
- Take medicines at the same times each day.
- Do physical activity about the same times each day.

No-Calorie Sweeteners

There's no need to dump no-calorie sweeteners just because sugar is safer than once thought. Sweeteners are "free foods" in your meal plan—and that's a good thing! They make foods taste sweet, they have no calories, and they won't raise your blood glucose levels. The following sweeteners are accepted by the Food and Drug Administration as safe to eat: aspartame (Equal and NutraSweet), acesulfame potassium (Sweet One), saccharin (Sweet'N Low and Sugar Twin), and sucralose (Splenda).

Basic carbohydrate counting relies on eating about the same amount of carbohydrates at the same times each day to keep blood glucose levels in your target range. It's a good meal-planning method if you have type 2 diabetes and take no daily oral diabetes medications or take one to two shots of insulin per day.

Advanced carbohydrate counting is a more complex method than the basic system of carbohydrate counting. It's designed for individuals who take multiple daily insulin injections or use an insulin pump. With advanced carbohydrate counting, you have to balance the amount of carbohydrates you consume with the insulin you take. You estimate the amount of carbohydrates you'll be eating and adjust your mealtime insulin dose based on your recommended insulin-to-carbohydrate ratio. To learn how to follow advanced carbohydrate counting, seek the assistance of a registered dietitian or certified diabetes educator.

Include Carbohydrates

Although the calories from fat, protein, and carbohydrate all affect your blood glucose level, carbohydrates affect it the most. So why not just avoid carbohydrates altogether? While carbohydrates may be the main nutrient that raises blood glucose levels, you shouldn't cut them from your diet. Foods that contain carbohydrates are among the most healthful available—vegetables, fruits, whole grains, and low-fat or nonfat dairy foods. Eliminating these foods could compromise your health.

Be a Sugar Sleuth

Knowing the different forms of sugar can make life sweeter when you're reading labels and recipes. Sugar content is included in the total grams we list for carbohydrates in recipes.

- Sucrose appears in table sugar, molasses, beet sugar, brown sugar, cane sugar, powdered sugar, raw sugar, turbinado, and maple syrup.
- Other "-ose" sugars include glucose (or dextrose), fructose, lactose, and maltose. Fructose and sugar alcohols affect blood glucose less than sucrose, but large amounts of fructose may increase blood fat levels.
- Sugar alcohols such as sorbitol, xylitol, maltitol, mannitol, lactitol, and erythritol should only be eaten in moderation because they can cause diarrhea, gas, and cramping.

Be Sugar Smart

For many years, people with diabetes were told to shun sugar because it was thought that sugar caused blood glucose to soar out of control. So they diligently wiped sugary foods and sugar out of their diets, hoping to stabilize their blood glucose levels. Today, more than a dozen studies have shown sugars in foods don't cause blood glucose to spike any higher or faster than starches, such as those in potatoes and bread. The American Diabetes Association's recommendations on sugar now state "scientific evidence has shown that the use of sucrose (table sugar) as part of the meal plan does not impair blood glucose control in individuals with type 1 or type 2 diabetes."

It is important to note, however, that sugar is not a "free food." It still contains calories and offers no nutritional value beyond providing energy. So when you eat foods that contain sugar, they have to replace other carbohydrate-rich foods in your meal plan. Carbohydrates can contain a healthful amount of vitamins, minerals, and fiber. So it's a good idea to focus on whole grains and vegetables for your carbohydrates rather than sugar. Talk to your dietitian to determine a healthful way to include a moderate amount of sugar in your meal plan. Or you can sweeten foods with sugar substitutes (see "No-Calorie Sweeteners," *page 151*).

Stay Involved and Informed

Eating healthfully, exercising, and monitoring blood glucose levels help keep diabetes in check—all easier to do if you follow the plans you've developed with your health care providers. Update them on your progress and request changes if something isn't working. And stay informed about diabetes by going to *DiabeticLivingOnline.com* to sign up for our e-mail newsletter. You're the one who can monitor your progress day by day.

Using Our Nutrition Information

At the end of every one of our recipes, you'll see the nutrition information listed for each serving. You'll find the amount of calories (cal.), total fat, saturated fat (sat. fat), cholesterol (chol.), sodium, total carbohydrates (carb.), fiber, and protein (pro.). In addition, you'll find the number of diabetic exchanges for each serving and the number of carbohydrate choices, in case you prefer those methods to keep track of what you're eating.

Interpreting the Numbers

Use our nutrition analyses to keep track of the nutritional values of the foods you eat, following the meal plan you and your dietitian have decided is right for you. Refer to that plan to see how a recipe fits the number of diabetic exchanges or carbohydrate choices you're allotted for each day. When you try a recipe, jot down our nutrition numbers to keep a running tally of what you're eating, remembering your daily allowances. At the end of each day, see how your numbers compare with your plan.

Diabetic Exchanges

The exchange system allows you to choose from a variety of items within several food groupings. Those groupings include starch, fruit, fat-free milk, carbohydrates, nonstarchy vegetables, meat and meat substitutes, fat, and free foods. To use the diabetic exchange system with our recipes, follow your plan's recommendations on the number of servings you should select from each exchange group in a day.

Carbohydrate Counting

Our recipes help you keep track of carbohydrates in two ways—tallying grams of carbohydrates and the number of carbohydrate choices. For counting grams, add the amounts of total carbohydrates to your running total for the day. For carbohydrate choices, one choice equals 15 grams of carbohydrates. For example, a sandwich made with two slices of bread is 2 carbohydrate choices. The benefit of this system is that you're keeping track of small numbers.

Calculating Method

To calculate our nutrition information and offer flexibility in our recipes, we've made some decisions about what's included in our analyses and what's not. We follow these guidelines when we analyze recipes that list ingredient options or serving suggestions:

- When ingredient choices appear (such as yogurt or sour cream), we use the first one mentioned for the analysis.
- When an ingredient is listed as optional, such as a garnish or a suggested serve-along, we don't include it in our nutrition analysis.
- When we offer a range in the number of servings, we use the smaller number.
- For marinades, we assume most of it is discarded.

recipe index

C

R

S

metric information

The charts on this page provide a guide for converting measurements from the U.S. customary system, which is used throughout this book, to the metric system.

Product Differences

Most of the ingredients called for in the recipes in this book are available in most countries. However, some are known by different names. Here are some common American ingredients and their possible counterparts:

* All-purpose flour is enriched, bleached or unbleached white household flour. When self-rising flour is used in place of all-purpose flour in a recipe that calls for leavening, omit the leavening agent (baking soda or baking powder) and salt.
* Baking soda is bicarbonate of soda.
* Cornstarch is cornflour.
* Golden raisins are sultanas.
* Light-colored corn syrup is golden syrup.
* Powdered sugar is icing sugar.
* Sugar (white) is granulated, fine granulated, or castor sugar.
* Vanilla or vanilla extract is vanilla essence.

Volume and Weight

The United States traditionally uses cup measures for liquid and solid ingredients. The chart below shows the approximate imperial and metric equivalents. If you are accustomed to weighing solid ingredients, the following approximate equivalents will be helpful.

* 1 cup butter, castor sugar, or rice = 8 ounces = 1/2 pound = 250 grams
* 1 cup flour = 4 ounces = 1/4 pound = 125 grams
* 1 cup icing sugar = 5 ounces = 150 grams

Canadian and U.S. volume for a cup measure is 8 fluid ounces (237 ml), but the standard metric equivalent is 250 ml.

1 British imperial cup is 10 fluid ounces.

In Australia, 1 tablespoon equals 20 ml, and there are 4 teaspoons in the Australian tablespoon.

Spoon measures are used for smaller amounts of ingredients. Although the size of the tablespoon varies slightly in different countries, for practical purposes and for recipes in this book, a straight substitution is all that's necessary. Measurements made using cups or spoons always should be level unless stated otherwise.

Common Weight Range Replacements

Imperial / U.S.	Metric
1/2 ounce	15 g
1 ounce	25 g or 30 g
4 ounces (1/4 pound)	115 g or 125 g
8 ounces (1/2 pound)	225 g or 250 g
16 ounces (1 pound)	450 g or 500 g
1 1/4 pounds	625 g
1 1/2 pounds	750 g
2 pounds or 2 1/4 pounds	1,000 g or 1 Kg

Oven Temperature Equivalents

Fahrenheit Setting	Celsius Setting*	Gas Setting
300°F	150°C	Gas Mark 2 (very low)
325°F	160°C	Gas Mark 3 (low)
350°F	180°C	Gas Mark 4 (moderate)
375°F	190°C	Gas Mark 5 (moderate)
400°F	200°C	Gas Mark 6 (hot)
425°F	220°C	Gas Mark 7 (hot)
450°F	230°C	Gas Mark 8 (very hot)
475°F	240°C	Gas Mark 9 (very hot)
500°F	260°C	Gas Mark 10 (extremely hot)
Broil	Broil	Grill

*Electric and gas ovens may be calibrated using celsius. However, for an electric oven, increase celsius setting 10 to 20 degrees when cooking above 160°C. For convection or forced air ovens (gas or electric), lower the temperature setting 25°F/10°C when cooking at all heat levels.

Baking Pan Sizes

Imperial / U.S.	Metric
9×1 1/2-inch round cake pan	22- or 23×4-cm (1.5 L)
9×1 1/2-inch pie plate	22- or 23×4-cm (1 L)
8×8×2-inch square cake pan	20×5-cm (2 L)
9×9×2-inch square cake pan	22- or 23×4.5-cm (2.5 L)
11×7×1 1/2-inch baking pan	28×17×4-cm (2 L)
2-quart rectangular baking pan	30×19×4.5-cm (3 L)
13×9×2-inch baking pan	34×22×4.5-cm (3.5 L)
15×10×1-inch jelly roll pan	40×25×2-cm
9×5×3-inch loaf pan	23×13×8-cm (2 L)
2-quart casserole	2 L

U.S. / Standard Metric Equivalents

1/8 teaspoon = 0.5 ml	
1/4 teaspoon = 1 ml	
1/2 teaspoon = 2 ml	
1 teaspoon = 5 ml	
1 tablespoon = 15 ml	
2 tablespoons = 25 ml	
1/4 cup = 2 fluid ounces = 50 ml	
1/3 cup = 3 fluid ounces = 75 ml	
1/2 cup = 4 fluid ounces = 125 ml	
2/3 cup = 5 fluid ounces = 150 ml	
3/4 cup = 6 fluid ounces = 175 ml	
1 cup = 8 fluid ounces = 250 ml	
2 cups = 1 pint = 500 ml	
1 quart = 1 litre	